		VAT REG	677 3993 86	Customer No. 0001950382		Delivery No. 8001328553		Despatch Date 14/11/09
		CO. REG.	2125768	Order No. 0004677952		Date of Order 13/11/09		Media Code : EKT1

Description	Size	Disc	Price	Qty	Item No.	Invoice	Code	
Easy Care Blazer, Navy, 40"		£0.00	£32.19	1	AD1028015			
31 F/F Care Trouser, Navy, 38"		£0.00	£13.79	1	AC10494012			
MENS STRETCH JEANS 32" , BLS, 38		£0.00	£16.08	1	C634G-BLS-38			4
MENS STRETCH JEANS, Light Stonewash, 38		£0.00	£16.09	1	C634G-LSW-38			80
								1221
								04

Listed above are your delivery details

Discount	£0.00
VAT @ 15%	£10.71
Handling & Insurance	£3.99
Payment received with thanks	£82.14

CW00430246

RETURNS LABEL How to use: Peel off and attach the returns label below to the outsic

PEEL HERE

Please tick service to be used

Cotton Traders

P.O. BOX 1311

BRADFORD

BD5 5AQ

0002186027

CUSTOMER DETAILS
Dr N Morris
59 Westbourne Road, Penn
WOLVERHAMPTON
West Midlands
West Midlands
WV4 5UF

DELIVERY ADDRESS
Dr N Morris
59 Westbourne Road, Penn
WOLVERHAMPTON
West Midlands
West Midlands
WV4 5UF

Cotton Traders are committed to deliver a world class, customer focused service that meets the needs of all our customers. Our aim is to provide quality contemporary clothing at affordable prices. We aim to provide clothing that continues to look, fit, and feel good after every wash.

RETURNS INFORMATION

We want you to be happy with every purchase, but if you need to return an item it's as easy as A B C. Please see details below. If you need to contact us we are here to help on 0844 844 1111 and there's more information at cottontraders.co.uk too. We are happy to refund in full, for any unworn item within 7 days or for faulty goods received - just follow the steps below.

A - Complete the Returns slip below and pop it into your parcel
B - Peel off the label overleaf and fix to your parcel - note that this is not a pre paid label
C - Take the parcel to any post office

Refunds

All orders returned back to Cotton Traders are automatically refunded back to the original payment method account.

EXCHANGES

If you would like a replacement item (alternative size or colour) we will re-order with no fee to you for post and packing - please call us on 0844 844 1111 and quote EXCH.

Frequently asked questions

Why do I have to pay for returns?

We do not offer free returns because we aim to keep the cost of the product as low as possible. If you need an alternative size or colour, we will happily send a replacement product out free of charge of postage. If goods are found to be faulty we do reimburse any costs incurred.

Where is my refund?

Refunds are processed on receipt with payment credited to your original payment method account. Payment will take 3 days to be credited from receipt of return. If you paid by postal order we will refund by cheque. Delays will occur if the returns slip is incomplete or not included in your return parcel.

How do I know you have received my return?

Our operators will be able to confirm if your return has been received - however we do recommend you keep proof of postage and consider parcel insurance when you send your items back to us. Please note that Cotton Traders are not liable for any parcels damaged or lost in transit when being returned.

Please complete the Returns Note below, indicating your reasons for return, detach and return inside the parcel.

A - Faulty/Poor quality   B - Not liked   C - Too long   D - Too short   E - Too big   F - Too small
G - Fabric/Material   H - Colour   J - Ordered for Choice   K - Incorrect Item Received   M - Arrived too late

RETURNS NOTE

Description	Size	Invoice	Item No.	Qty	Reason for return code	Warehouse use only
Easy Care Blazer, Navy, 40"			AD1028S015			
31 F/F Care Trouser, Navy, 38"			AC10494012			
MENS STRETCH JEANS 32", BLS, 38			C634G-BLS-38			
MENS STRETCH JEANS, Light Stonewash, 38			C634G-LSW-38			

detach and return inside parcel   TOTAL ITEMS RETURNED

If any item received in your delivery differs from that stated above please use this space to indicate the correct item details

Dr N Morris
Customer No.
0001950382

Date of Order
13/11/09

Customer
signature _____

Date _____

Customer No. 0001950382

Invoice	Item No.	Tick Returned Items
	AD1028S015	
	AC10494012	
	C634G-BLS-38	
	C634G-LSW-38	

E D

0002186027

1017

About the Author

Ali Ansari was born in India where he did his undergraduate work in Mechanical Engineering. He moved to the USA in 1969 and received a Ph.D. in Mechanical Engineering from the University of Florida in 1973. Since then he has taught at several universities in USA, Nigeria and India and has coauthored a textbook on thermodynamics, published by John Wiley & Sons.

Ansari is also a literary writer and poet and his work has appeared in several magazines. Ansari began developing his ideas and vision of the New Sufi system as a powerful synthesis of Eastern and Western knowledge aimed at a very deep level of personal insight and transformation after being associated with a number of teachers in the East and the West. Much of the New Sufi material is however based on his own original and personal work and the workshops and classes he frequently conducts. He can be reached at aliansari@vsnl.com

First Published in India
in 1999 by
Mapin Publishing Pvt. Ltd.
31, Somnath Road, Usmanpura
Ahmedabad 380013 India
mapinpub@vsnl.com
www.mapinpub.com

Simultaneously published in the
United States of America in 2000 by
Grantha Corporation
80 Cliffedgeway, Middletown, NJ 07701

Distributed in North America by
Antique Collectors' Club
Market Street Industrial Park
Wappingers' Falls, NY 12590
Tel: 800-252-5231
Fax: 914-297-0068
email: info@antiquecc.com
www.antiquecc.com

Distributed in the United Kingdom & Europe by
Antique Collectors' Club
5 Church Street, Woodbridge
Suffolk IP12 1DS, UK
Tel: 1394 385 501
Fax: 1394 384 434
email: accvs@aol.com

Text © Ali Ansari
Cover photo © Sukut-i-Shab by
Abdul Rehman Chughtai
Courtesy: HEART, Bombay

ISBN: 81-85822-72-7 (Mapin)
ISBN: 1-890206-23-7 (Grantha)
LC: 99-76988

Edited by: Mallika Sarabhai
Editorial Consultant: Krishen Kak
Designed by: Mapin Design Studio
Printed by: Thompson Press, Faridabad, India

Sufism and Beyond

Sufi Thought in the Light of Late 20th Century Science

Ali Ansari

Mapin Publishing Pvt. Ltd., Ahmedabad

A Note to the Reader

I don't know what spectrum of readers this book is going to enjoy. I have in mind an "average" reader who is sensitive to the spiritual quest and is curious about it in a healthy sort of way. Practically the entire book is about understanding the spiritual quest. To do this I have drawn rather strongly on certain concepts in science and psychology. I have kept the discussion of scientific facts somewhat general and relatively simple. My interest is in understanding certain broad features of the human brain, with particular emphasis on spirituality. I believe rather strongly that the spiritual drive is an evolutionary drive and it is extremely important for us to understand it. The book is therefore a bridge between contemporary science and authentic insights of spiritual teachers into the human mind. How does the brain conceive the self? How does it conceive the "other"? Why does it perceive the world as a collection of separate objects? Is it possible to eliminate fear? These are legitimate questions for science and psychology and they also lie at the heart of the spiritual quest. I should be satisfied if this book leads you by way of the mind to your heart. In some chapters, e.g., the Introduction and Chapter 1, there may be passages that seem complex or too philosophical. It is perfectly all right to run through them lightly. It is sufficient if one gets the general drift of the argument. I wish to lead you to a deep understanding of the spiritual impulse and I believe that this can be done through a combination of scientific insight and mystic knowledge. To facilitate this, I have given a brief overview of the chapter at the outset of selected chapters.

A word about the organisation of the material. I wrote Parts I and II first and then tacked on Part III and the opening section, including the Introduction. The arrangement is therefore like a musical composition, more circular than linear. In the Introduction many conclusions are stated. But one must follow the complete thought process in Parts I, II and III before judging the validity of the conclusions.

A Sufi Hymn to Awareness

Neither subject nor object, neither seer nor seen
Awareness is a flame which glows into itself

For those who have the eyes, for those who wish to see
It opens its heart and shows into itself

Neither here nor there, its home is nowhere
Like a wind it blows and blows into itself

Beginning with a drop in each moment of Creation
It soon becomes a river that flows into itself

From where does it come and to where does it go?
Like a breath it comes and goes into itself

To nothing does it submit, 'cause nothing's other than it
To itself it bows, as it bows to itself

Dedicated

To the unknown lineage, for ongoing help

To Murshid Isa, for kindling the fire

and

to Yo: I didn't understand what you were trying to teach me

until life, through much pain, forced me to learn it for

myself

Contents

Acknowledgments

A writing project like this one requires resources beyond one person's individual capacities. Many people provided direct and indirect help. The Coimbatore group of counsellors at the Centre For Holistic Integrated Learning And Development, under the management of P.K. Saru, frequently served as a captive audience as I gave seminars and workshops over a two-year period to give shape and substance to New Sufi thought. I wish to thank them for their interest and support. Fanita English, psychotherapist and psychological theorist, followed with keen interest the evolution of New Sufi thought and offered valuable suggestions. Many family members, Saru, Amy, Unni, Javeed, to name a few, helped immensely with their empathy, interest and love. My debt to my wife, Aysha, is deep and abiding. She was always there, with her silent, comforting presence, concern and support and uncanny intuition about when to leave me alone with my computer and when to come to my rescue.

My publisher and editor at Mapin, Bipin Shah and Mallika Sarabhai, helped in numerous ways by tuning in to the subtle as well as the manifest in the book. Without them, and Paulomi Shah's lovely design work, the book might have fallen far short of its present form. My friend, Jaishree Varadaraj, not only brought me together with Bipin and Mallika but also helped in many other ways.

Through the numerous "encounter group" workshops I gave in Coimbatore and Bangalore, I learnt a thing or two about love which practically transformed my inner and outer lives. Together, we crossed forbidden barriers and took a few decisive steps towards discovering what is real and what is not.

Preface

One of the joys of writing a preface is that it is the last thing one writes, even though it appears first in the book. As I write this, I have before me a bird's-eye view of the book. Throughout the writing I felt that I was solving some kind of a deep puzzle. Have I solved it?

Evolutionary biology has been marvellously successful in fitting together all the major pieces of our evolutionary past. It has revealed to us the mechanics of biological evolution. All organisms on earth have a common ancestry. Many more organisms are produced than can be supported by the natural food base of a particular environment. Natural selection acts on random genetic mutations and allows the fittest to survive, yielding thereby the dynamics of evolution. This is how, as a species of higher primates, we have come into being. However, our remarkable cognitive resources have made it possible for us to master our environment. We have effectively put natural selection out of action.

So what's going to govern our *future* evolution? Our evolution as a species? Evolutionary biology fails us here. And what about *personal* evolution? There is no such concept in biology. Yet, each one of us knows very well that there is such a thing as personal growth. And that it is exciting and wonderful to pursue and experience. There are signs all around us that human society is entering an "Age of Personal Growth". Having more or less solved, as a species, the problems of biological survival, the drama of evolution for us has shifted to the personal and the individual.

What sort of personal growth do we wish to undergo? What does it mean to be truly human? Science can be of little help in answering this question. Some other form of knowing is required.

Not knowledge, but a knowing that is never static, never complete. It is not found in books or teachings. This knowing tells us that it is for us now to transform our primate-human brain, for this brain has become for us, individually and collectively, a source of conflict and suffering.

Sufism, like many other similar systems, guides us in evolving a *metaprimate* brain. By combining Sufi knowledge and methods with modern discoveries in science we may not only understand the roots of primate fear and greed and insecurity in our psyche but also learn how to transform them.

The Sufi doctrine maintains that there is, in our psyche, a natural and powerful urge to expand continuously towards a point of ultimate freedom. And that freedom is freedom from the dichotomy of ME and THOU. I believe that it is time for science and psychology to understand this spiritual drive, which is a personal evolutionary drive, and honour it.

How can we set ourselves free? The mystics and the sages try to teach us. But their teachings are couched in strange metaphors. This book is a re-statement of those teachings in the light of late 20th century science. The work of setting oneself free is personal and individual. Everyone has to do it for himself. But it helps to understand clearly what we are intuitively trying to do. And to know how and where to tap the necessary resources.

The Mystery of Spiritual Longing

The water-drop's bliss is to merge with the sea
Pain, crossing its limits, becomes its own remedy

(a couplet by Ghalib, translated from Urdu)

What does the poet wish to convey through the metaphor of the water-drop's merging with the ocean? According to Sufi philosophy, the human soul harbours within itself a deep anguish—the anguish of the separate self. This distress drives it towards liberation—the point where the self no longer experiences itself as a separate self.

What do these terms mean—liberation, enlightenment, self-realisation, maya, spiritual longing? What is the soul? Does it exist and, if so, in what sense, how and where? What is non-dual consciousness—the state of mind of the self-realised sage? Can mystic/spiritual teachings and psychology and the new emerging neurosciences be made to speak to each other? I believe they can in a powerful way—powerful enough to fundamentally alter our view of the world.

Overview: In this opening section I have introduced "the problem", or rather the set of problems which relate spirituality to biology and psychology. How does the sense of Self arise? How does the brain conceive the Self? Is the Self "real"or an "artifact"? What does spirituality have to do with the reality or unreality of the Self? With spiritual growth the dichotomy of Me and Thou begins to soften. How does this relate to the structure of the primate-human mind and its evolution towards a metaprimate mind? These seemingly philosophical questions are also intensely personal for those deeply involved in the process of spiritual growth.

We are the curtain that lies between
Without us who would hide from whom?

A Sufi couplet by Mir, translated from Urdu

Remember picture puzzles? I don't know what the new generation of computer literate four-year olds thinks of them, but I still find them fascinating and can't help thinking strange philosophical thoughts about the rules which go into their making and doing. The makers, it seems to me, are nice guys. At least, to the kids. The puzzles are made to fit. The child takes this on faith and is never let down.

There are several other things that I find interesting about picture puzzles. They have a neat closure. The final picture, usually a composite scene of several objects, is easy to cognise and has a strong eidetic dimension, with a variety of colours and familiar shapes. It is invariably engaging. The pieces are all smoothly contoured and made to fit snugly. Might we say that assembling a puzzle is a character-building exercise? It implicitly teaches the child, or rather reassures it, that things are made to work out.

The validity of the assumption when applied to life is, of course, questionable. It is natural enough that the child would, from picture building and many similar geometrical and educational toys, arrive subconsciously at certain generalisations. That life makes sense. That somebody—the maker of life (like the puzzle manufacturer) is reasonable and intelligent and presents to us (creatures) challenges and problems which have solutions.

If we were to take a moment to think about it, this is a rather fantastic and crucial set of beliefs. It sets the tone of the human mind's relationship to the perceptible and *imperceptible* universe. What doesn't seem complete on the perceptible level is made whole by invoking the imperceptible. In the final analysis, it is the human mind's relationship with the imperceptible, more than that with the perceptible, that gives human existence its peculiar flavour.

Let me switch now to an account of a personal odyssey that began when I was eleven. I am not sure just how the urge to solve the "puzzle of life" took hold in my mind. What made me think (feel?) that life is a puzzle and, further, that the puzzle is solvable? Was it an unconscious reference to puzzle games and some implicit faith (knowing?) that somehow at some level it all makes sense? It was only some twenty years later that I consciously caught on to the idea that in my mind I was merely putting together pieces to make a big "logical" picture, but the logic didn't seem to be a human artifact (1). The mind, the right brain perhaps, appeared to be responding to some form of apprehension that seemed almost objective. A sense of geometry? A grand aesthetic sensibility? Is the universe really inherently harmonious? Or, is it only the human mind that is so? And does the sense of harmony emanate from the mind's relationship to the imperceptible? The grand logical pattern woven by the formulations of physics suggests a breathtaking harmony linking matter and energy—a reasonableness to the universe we have no fundamental right to expect. Or do we? Is there a mind lurking behind it all? Perhaps our own mind? "The stuff of the universe is mind-stuff", declared physicist A.S. Eddington(2).

1 Ansari, A., *Higher-order Energy And Information Spaces: A Conceptual Framework* (privately published, 1979).
2 Eddington, A.S., *The Nature of the Physical World* (Macmillan, 1928).

What then might one say about meaning? A fanciful creation of the human mind? Years after studying physics and engineering, I got interested in biology. And eventually the neurosciences. It was a thrill I would not easily forget. At last, the puzzle of life, and even that of human existence, took on the form of a series of closely related, well-posed questions. From the cell to the brain to the huge overall society of cells called the body, a dazzlingly complex but inherently orderly set of physical and chemical processes appears to govern the physical and mental functioning of every organism. There is, it appears, no more meaning to life than the will of the genes to self-perpetuate. And this will itself is, by all indications, a chemical phenomenon, ultimately explainable in terms of the laws of physics. At least, this is how it all seems to be.

But a problem arises. How did these laws originate? There is absolutely nothing in the framework of the laws to indicate, let alone tell, from where they have come. So philosophers of science question the question. The question, they say, presumes a more or less linear ordering in time. But what if time itself has no particular reality? To quote Eddington again: "We found a strange footprint in the sands of time. We looked far and wide for the creature to which it belonged. When we found that creature, Lo! it was us."

A Sufi poet says:
My mind is a prisoner of qualities and names
And Reality has no qualities, no name.

(translated from Urdu)

What is "Reality" and what is artifact? How would one tell? Science has no means to decide what is real and what is an artifact. Because, to do so means asking whether science itself is real or an artifact. And this science cannot ask and answer using its own resources.

This apparent dead-end is met in a more curious manner in biology. At the heart of Darwinian/Neo-Darwinian thought is the proposition that the gene compulsively replicates "itself". Regardless of whether this is traced to a basic explanation in terms of the chemistry and physics of self-replicating molecular chains, the question of how the organism, whether a single cell or a trillion-trillion cell creature, makes the crucial distinction between self and non-self opens a Pandora's box of riddles there is absolutely no way to close.

This fascinating question takes one off on a tangent concerning sense-perception, measurement, instrumentation, etc. Apparently the cell and the multitrillion cell organism sense their own physical and chemical boundary and form. However, in what seems to be a rigmarole reminiscent of the Uncertainty Principle, the boundary is an *artifact* of the sensing mechanism— its resolution power and other design parameters. For example, a blind person establishes distinctions between solid objects through touch. If both her hands are paralyzed or become entirely numb and the sense of touch is completely lost, the ability to tell objects apart would fail. This does not mean that the person would have no sense of physical self. This sense is genetically programmed into the processes of the brain and the chemical/physical "image" of the body would persist within the brain even in the absence of input from peripheral sensors. Yet it is obvious that as a physical system the organism is limited by design parameters. Many bacteria and viruses use devious means to confuse the host organism and invade it with immunity. To do this they take advantage of the limitations of the host organism's self-sensing apparatus.

It is therefore clear that the distinction between self and other is relative and not absolute. It is a manifestation of the basic measurement problem, as well as a matter of detail concerning fidelity, precision and operation of the sense-perception system.

This insight into the relationship between the system's hardware, its engineering parameters and ultimately, its "consciousness" suggested a new approach to the solution of the basic puzzle. Sensing has little meaning without perception. The products of perception are mental *artifacts*. We might call them "cognifacts". How does the brain achieve perception? It is evident, both from arguments of physics and experimental data in psychology concerning visual perception (see Chapter 1), that perception is invariably selective. The brain sees selectively, as the difference between the words *seeing* and *looking* indicates. (In many languages, especially English, there are many words and phrases which relate cognition to visual perception, e.g. obvious, evident, insight, observations, views, depends on how you look at it, I see!).

If perception is selective, what *biases* are involved in determining what is perceived and what is not? The question is explored in some detail in Chapter 1. In a nutshell, however, it appears to come down to a question of values. The organism perceives according to need. The driving compulsion is necessarily survival. The organism values itself. And what, we might ask, is this "itself"? The answer in the case of all except the highest level of primates is the physico-chemical self—the "body", which is a container housing a vast complex of chemically (genetically) unique cells.

At this point, the pieces of the puzzle fell together. By introducing the insight concerning selective sensing into the neo-Darwinian framework most of the loose ends appeared to tie up.

I realised, however, that other, more profound, questions are raised which go beyond this framework. The most important, and the least abstract, of these is: what guides the evolution of an organism, or a species of organisms, *for whom physical survival is no longer a practical issue*? In the last ten or fifteen thousand years we have achieved a level of control over the natural environment which has rendered this issue—the most crucial and consuming issue for other organisms, something of a non-issue in our case. What is to drive *our* future evolution?

Suddenly, one is forced to look beyond matter and energy. And beyond Neo-Darwinian thought. For thousands of years sages of the East have spoken of another type of evolution. Evolution of the "spirit", they called it—but the term is not important. *The essence of this teaching is that something drives human consciousness on an evolutionary course that is remarkably different from that identified by Darwinian thought—a course that is perhaps one hundred and eighty degrees in relation to it.* They called this course "annihilation of self".

The mystery continued to deepen as I pondered the puzzle with a growing sense of wonder. There were, indeed, many outstanding pieces in the realm of human experience completely at odds with the picture drawn by evolutionary biology. Despite the fact that evolutionary biology has had spectacular success in neatly fitting together a vast amount of data concerning biological evolution, it has nothing significant to say about the evolution of human consciousness—or the evolution of the human mind, individual or collective.

The poverty of the framework of evolutionary biology gradually became clear. There is simply no way to meaningfully place the course of future human evolution in it. There are no signposts, nothing to direct future "traffic", as it were. In a scenario in which the human species has achieved a permanently stable global population and a vast technological network of immense power, natural selection—the force that has brought our species where it now stands, is rendered moot. (This may lead to bizarre possibilities as the following amusing passage in Encyclopaedia Britannica 1998 indicates:
"As technology develops, natural selection enters new behavioural arenas; for example, in an age of artificial contraception, the clumsy and forgetful preferentially reproduce.")

Some evolutionary biologists believe that various forms of environmental selection will replace natural selection and may influence evolution and patterns of reproduction in unpredictable ways. Culture might play a major role in selecting out "the fittest". Certainly, the process of achieving social and economic success is an important driving force in the evolution of the individual human mind. To a very considerable extent, culture determines the values which motivate human endeavour and growth. If we were simple biological organisms our activities might be said to be guided by the avoidance of physical pain and the seeking of pleasure. However, human suffering goes beyond physical pain and I don't believe evolutionary psychology can explain its complexities.

It is at this point that a crossroads is reached and we are forced to consider the claim of the mystic or the "self-realised". There is indeed an overall directing force to human life and human consciousness, says the mystic. It is the seeking of a remedy for a kind of pain peculiar to the human "soul". What is this pain and what is it about? Where lies its remedy? Almost all Urdu Sufi poetry is concerned with this two-sided question. The poet Ghalib answers thus:

> The water-drop's bliss is to merge with the sea
> Pain, crossing its limits, becomes its own remedy

> (translated from Urdu)

Separateness of self from other selves, and ultimately the Universal Self, is the elemental source of human suffering. As long as the self remains attached to its own (imagined) reality, it is driven by fear, need for self-protection, desire, want, competitive struggle, and so on. Out of this is born the spark of spiritual suffering which seeks its own consummation in the merging of the individual self with the Universal Self.

> Here is what Ghalib has to say:
> To the degree that I believe in the reality of "the other"
> Am I removed from my own reality

The elements of New Sufi thought began to emerge with clarity at this point. It seems to come down in the end to a basic question of valuation, or relative "weighing" of choices. Bad or wrong or false valuation causes suffering. To sustain a constant illusion one must have access to a vast set of biological, cultural and psychological devices to go on deceiving oneself. These are provided by false valuation. For example, if we invest in war then we must, at great expense and effort, manufacture a vast arsenal to wage war. Not only this, we must manufacture fear and greed and acquisitiveness and singleminded desire to win. A guaranteed recipe for suffering. If, on the other hand, we invest in peace, then everything is taken care of. Everyone "wins".

Mystic thought aims at a fundamental correction of wrong valuation. To value an illusion is poor investment. Gautama, the Buddha, though he would object to being called a mystic, taught this in a unique way to his monks, using a method that involved direct transmission of insight. (Who coined the term, mystic? What a travesty of the extraordinary clarity of sight which the mystic enjoys!) To want to hold on to the illusion of a fixed self—the personal self, in the midst of a reality of continuous change is like trading the living life for a snapshot. With absolutely no benefit of access to objective knowledge about the processes of the brain, the Buddha realised that the brain manufactures continuity! It is not unlike the mechanics of a motion picture, in which a succession of photographic stills is exhibited to the eye so quickly that it "experiences" movement of the picture—merely an optical illusion created by the physical characteristics of the visual sensing and perceptual apparatus. As an object and product of perception, the apparent reality of a fixed "personal" self might, in the language of 20th century science, be called a neurally orchestrated illusion. The Buddha' s teaching method involved replacing this natural experiential illusion with a dazzling insight into discontinuous reality. (More about the Buddha's method, and Sufi teaching methods, later.)

It is easy to appreciate why "self-realisation" is so very rare and virtually impossible to achieve by intentional effort. It is unnatural. When it happens it is virtually a neural event. Normal perceptual circuits are snapped. The neural programming that holds the personal self together as a psychological icon of personal devotion and investment is undone. Not surprisingly, most accounts of experiences of self-realisation speak of the "influence" of a self-realised master or Guru. The interaction is infinitely subtle, quite possibly a neural "quantum" event triggered by a consciousness field or vibration[1].

This is a good place to highlight the special features of New Sufi thought. It will be seen that it draws heavily and deeply on mystic teachings on the one hand and late 20th century science, on the other. The result is a reconciliation of science and authentic mystic insight and experience into a single conceptual framework that draws as much on physics, psychology, biology and the neurosciences as on spiritual teachings.

Another major feature is a reformulation of biological evolutionary thought in the light of insights into the design characteristics of organic sense perceptual systems. The fundamental sanctity of the personal self from the point of view of the mind hinges on a perceptually established "physical" boundary of one's own body. This is an artifact. Alter the parameters of the sense-perception system and the boundary shifts. Mystics throughout the ages have spoken of the "unreality" of the world. What did they mean? Were they tipped off by something in their own consciousness that perception arises within the brain and is essentially a process of creating perceptual/cognitive artifacts? The insight was evidently based on an actual experience and encounter with the Formless—the Absolute. In this encounter the illusion of self is undone. To quote Ghalib again:

> Oh, fellow seekers, who wants to hear the cruel taunt of failure
> Seeing that HE is not to be found, I chose to lose myself.
>
> (translated from Urdu)

This book presents a theory of "relative reality" by making reference to neural processes. Reference is made to an ordering and organisation of sense data by the mind using a basic perceptual mould. In spiritual teachings this perceptual mould is called "duality". Duality appears to go hand-in-hand with a value system that holds the separation of self from non-self as a preferred mode of perception. The fact that in self-realisation both of these, the particular mould and the associated value system, are drastically and permanently altered indicates their close relationship. What seems to happen is that "investment" in a personal self is dissipated, and concomitantly, duality, or separation of self from the "other", is given up.

I believe that these seemingly nebulous "mystical" notions have a physical reality in the processes of the brain. I would hazard the guess that, along with a dramatic rewiring of neural connections, certain precise chemical reactions in specific synaptic clefts are involved in these radical and deeply abiding spiritual perceptions referred to as self-realisation[2]. The sense of a separate, personal self is certainly both biological, cultural and psychological. But the three are closely related. Many LSD-type drugs drastically alter the sense of ego or personal self by temporarily changing brain chemistry. However, self-realisation is usually a permanent, irreversible and drastic alteration of the normal human experience of duality. Psychologically, it has a wide set of correlates. Reports indicate that there is invariably a profound sense of peace, a total, permanent absence of anxiety, a constant feeling of fulfillment and sometimes, but not in every case, a sense of exhilaration and bliss.(There are also quite significant individual variations. I will comment on this later.) It is reasonable to presume that such a permanent altered state of consciousness is likely to involve a drastic alteration in brain and body chemistry, in addition to a re-synapsing of crucial neural connections.

However, one needs to go farther than this. There must be programmes, genetic or otherwise, which control neural chemistry and electrical activity. It is well-known that not only memories but also emotional reactions to memories are programmed in the brain in the form of neural pathways[3]. Fear, for example, as a specific emotional component of a particular memory, corresponds to very specific chemical and electrical activity within the brain. Presumably, so does love. Once again, experience with psychotropic drugs has clearly established this. The major mystery in the case of self-realisation, i.e. the permanent elimination of all sense of duality, is what exactly happens within the brain. Is some basic, "master" program corresponding to the normal human sense of duality radically altered and rewritten?

The questions become even more tantalising when we look at it from the standpoint of values. The sense of duality exists, and persists, in consciousness because it is valued (I presume this relative valuing also has a chemical/physical correlate, or is possibly a matter of "synaptic weighting".) That is, the self is valued above non-self. On a purely biological level the self means physical and chemical identity. "The gene is selfish", as one biologist has put it. Apparently, in self-realisation, or temporarily in a mystical experience, this basic value system is deeply affected on a psychological/emotional level. Is the "mind" of the gene also affected?

Mystics and sages maintain that human consciousness necessarily evolves in the direction of transcendence of duality. This, they say, is what spiritual "seeking"—the seeking of God or "truth", is all about. The dynamics of this evolution is supported

---

3 Le Doux, J.. *The Emotional Brain* (Simon & Schuster, 1996).

by a deeply intuitive drive for the elimination of the "natural anguish" of the personal self. This anguish derives from the creation of "me" in opposition to "thou". Consciousness appears to be pulled very subtly toward a final, stable "attractor state", a term coined by the physical-chemist, Ilya Prigogine, in a different context, and this attractor state is the psychological state of non-duality. The mystic has strong reason to claim that this is a "final" state of evolution, because when the state of non-duality is actualised there is a profound sense of completion and psychological release (liberation).

A schema is proposed in Chapter 6 to the effect that the human psyche is composed of two dialectically opposed systems—a "Self-Concern System" (SCS) and a "Self-Unconcern System" (SUS). The Self-Unconcern System is organised in a manner totally at odds with the fundamental assumptions of Darwinian thought. In operation, SUS is a progressive and systematic sabotage of SCS to set into motion the dynamics of human evolution to a "metaprimate" level.

Primate consciousness operates exclusively within the bounds of the Self-Concern System. The design characteristics of the primate mind and body, like that of all organisms, predispose consciousness towards a valuation of the unique physical/chemical entity it identifies as itself over other selves. In Part II, Chapters 7 to 9, is offered a series of arguments to the effect that given this self-identification (which appears to be an "arbitrary" choice made at the cellular level) and the fact that for the operation and propagation of life the organism *must* be biased in its own favour, the nature of the organism's interaction with the environment and with other organisms assumes the familiar character we see all around us. Life propagates itself, mindlessly producing organisms and inevitably pitching one organism against another. Struggle for existence is generated by scarcity of food.

In the last few thousand years the human species has decisively solved for itself the problem of simple physical existence. Certainly, there continue to be famine and drought and a certain level of permanent universal starvation as a result of economic deprivation. But the game of life for human beings has changed dramatically. What the human species is experiencing through its inexplicable agony is the birth pangs of the *metaprimate* mind and body.

> *I am completing myself,* says a Sufi poet, *A task left undone by God*

We are almost 100% primate in body and, on average, probably 90% primate in mind. And the other ten percent metaprimate mind is poorly integrated with the 90% primate mind.

There are, of course, great individual differences within the human spectrum. Some minds are discernibly more advanced in this evolutionary process. A crucial parameter in the process appears to be how the "self" is identified. If this identification is in material form there would always be a sense of scarcity and conflict. However, as we have seen, the identification itself is an artifact. The mind is predisposed by sensory design towards "material" identification of self in the form of a well-defined physical body. This is a consequence of a specific sensory and perceptual design. If, on the other hand, normal human senses could perceive energy fields over a large range of frequencies, identification of self with a well-defined spatial body would be difficult to sustain. As a matter of fact, the mind does *episense* to some extent, i.e. perceive signals outside the conscious range of perception. We pick up "vibes" from people and are profoundly, though unconsciously, influenced by our human and natural ambiance. However, conscious perception is usually dominated by focused sensory experience. As a result, we see the world as a chopped up collection of separate objects and separate and separated selves. (This will be explored further in Chapter 1.)

In Part III some detailed thoughts on the making of the metaprimate mind are offered. One important characteristic of such a mind is a shift outside the matter paradigm. The metaprimate mind and body (and soul) have the ability to feed on forms of nourishment radically different from those required by the primate mind and body. In as much as these are not material they are not limited by the calculus of scarcity. Love—

that enigmatic four-letter word, is an obvious example. In the balanced metaprimate mind the demands of the Self-Concern System and the Self-Unconcern System are healthily balanced.

What are the chances that the human species will be able to evolve sufficiently beyond the plane of primate consciousness before it causes great destruction and damage to itself and all life? The question is open-ended. Hope lies in the magnificent cognitive ability of the human mind to correlate cause and effect. Perhaps it would be able to sufficiently understand itself to solve its own problems of consciousness. Perhaps the instinct to seek relief from psychic suffering would help us overcome the primal passions, fears and compulsions of the primate mind. Perhaps science will discover the secrets of spirituality and learn to appreciate and honour them.

The writing of the book was dominated throughout by an uneasy mixture of hope and despair. I think what we see around us is a kind of advanced primate behaviour. This is cause for despair, considering the potential for destruction which science and technology have made available. Yet, by the same token, we may be poised on a threshold. And certainly, individually many people are involved in an extraordinary evolutionary process. It is a difficult place to be, when we are neither primate nor metaprimate. The absurdity and inappropriateness of many forms of primate thought, emotion and behaviour become evident to us and we struggle with these deeply programmed instincts and impulses. Slowly, with awareness, will and help, we evolve. I believe that at the core of human experience is the struggle to become metaprimate—a place where we don't own anything, not even what we consider to be *our* body.

Notes:

1. Neither biology, nor physics, nor a combination of the two, have so far been able to offer a scientifically acceptable explanation of consciousness. But many noteworthy attempts are under way. Some scientists seem to think that some type of coherent oscillations of neural circuits are involved in the physical mechanism of consciousness. The physicist Roger Penrose has been considering the problem by looking at the interface of quantum mechanics and classical mechanics. He believes

that some as yet undiscovered new physics applies at the interface and is relevant to the phenomenon of consciousness.

All such theories are still preliminary and speculative. However, the interesting thing is the real possibility of the existence of a consciousness field in a physical sense. Oscillations, certainly, could generate such a field and also cause transmission of information and energy. I believe that the mind routinely perceives in the episensory range and is influenced by episensory fields. We affect each other profoundly in an actual physical sense with or without overt sensory contact. I have very strong reason to believe this. The Sufis and enlightened beings of other such highly developed traditions consciously use these means and media of influence. Transmission of energy, knowledge and spiritual power through a lineage is a well-known phenomenon. It is also my firm understanding that our minds are influenced by suprasensory sources existing "outside the human plane". Interconnectedness is a natural consequence of the unity of creation. In fact, interconnectedness is a human concept, or an artifact, artificially superimposed on unity. It is perception which creates separate objects and the mind must then invent the concept of interconnectedness to simulate oneness. I will have more to say about this in Part III.

2. V.S. Ramachandran, a clinical neurologist, has written about the "mystical" experiences reported by some of his epileptic patients (4). His work is of particular interest because he has found an apparent correlation between "mystic" experiences and temporal lobe seizures. In his opinion the correlation is strong enough for him to propose, somewhat jokingly, the existence of a "God module" in the temporal lobes. "Does this syndrome imply that our brains contain some sort of circuitry that is actually specialised for religious experience?". "Most remarkable of all are those patients [of temporal lobe seizures] who have deeply moving spiritual experiences, including a feeling of divine presence and the sense that they are in direct communion with God. Everything around them is imbued with cosmic significance. They may say, 'I finally understand what it is all about. This is the moment I have been waiting for all my life.' Or, 'Finally I have insight into the true nature of the cosmos.' "

This clinical/empirical data has some bearing on my argument that decisive transformations like "enlightenment" probably involve some sort of drastic reorganisation of neural activity. I am, of course, not qualified to guess where such changes might be located within the brain. However, enlightenment, as I understand it, is not a religious "experience". It may or

---

4 Ramachandran, V.S. and Blakeslee, S., *Phantoms In The Brain* (4th Estate, 1998)

may not occur in the form of an experience. It is true that the term 'realisation' in 'self-realisation' has a ring of sudden insight, but to realise also means to achieve, or "convert into fact", as in "realise a hope or a plan" (Concise Oxford Dictionary). Self-realisation is a decisive and permanent transformation of cognition and feeling whereby, in some inexplicable sense, the normal human sense of me-thou dichotomy is erased. (I know of no way to say this in anything other than metaphoric language.) Just as no one, to my knowledge, has ever become self-realised through a drug-induced mystical experience, temporal lobe seizures may induce temporary mystical states, but to call them "God experiences" is obfuscation. (For what it is worth, one might make a distinction by saying that God is "realised", not experienced.)

What I have argued in this book is that there is an evolutionary drive in the human psyche to break out of the various ramifications of the me-thou dichotomy. The mind's sense of "the other" manifests in numerous ways, inducing it to restrict its circle of affection, include some and shut out others. With growth (emotional/spiritual), one's circle of affection expands. The point that I have made through systematic arguments is that the mind's sense of "me" or who "I" am is an artifact, a form of conceiving which depends on a lot of things. With spiritual growth, the "me" is continuously reconceived and the primate mind's basic mode of perception—self and "other", is gradually transformed.

Thoughts:
A Note about Sufi and New Sufi Thought

I must quickly make it clear that this book is only very indirectly about Sufism. It does not answer such questions as: What is Sufism? What is its message? Who "founded" it? What do the Sufis do? Who are the present Sufi teachers? My intent is to use some Sufi teachings and ideas to fill in certain important gaps in our knowledge of the human mind. New Sufi thought attempts to take up where both classical Sufism and contemporary science leave off. The reason is simple. Any serious attempt to make sense of the complete spectrum of human experience must integrate all, or many, of its elements into something approaching a whole. Art, science, spirituality, rationality, intuition, cognition, emotion—somewhere, at the top or at the bottom, all must meet.

The notion of the evolution of the primate-human mind into a metaprimate-human mind is by no means new.[1] What I have done is serve old wine in a new bottle. The wine, being old, has been tasted and passed by connoisseurs. It is to be hoped that the new bottle would not detract from its value.

I believe it is of critical importance that certain basic fallacies of science be corrected. *One of these is the identification of the human being as a material body with discernible boundaries and form, viz. those indicated by the visible human form.* This is an unfortunate and silly belief and ought to have been discarded long ago in the light of early 20th century discoveries in physics and the physiology of sense perception. It has led to the general belief

---

1   Scott, Ernst, *The People of the Secret* (Octagon Press, 1983).

at the heart of biology that we are distinct and separate entities, communicating and interacting with one another and the world only through obvious sensory channels—the limited frequencies of visible light, audible sound, etc.

Finally, I must comment on my choice of Sufi thought and Sufi work as a basic reference point. Unlike, say, Buddhist or Hindu or Taoist teachings, a great deal of Sufi work is centrally concerned with the transformation of the biological apparatus (2). It is intimately involved with matter and its relationship to energy and consciousness. A book by a contemporary Sufi teacher is evocatively titled, *The Human Biological Machine As a Transformational Apparatus.* Numerous features of Sufi philosophy to which I have made references in the book are features it shares with Buddhist and Hindu mystic thought. However, Sufi work takes these elements of thought and uses them to create a vision of an evolved human being—*Al Insanul Kamil*, the complete human being. This is not an abstract vision, or a vision of a superhuman being. Rather, it is a living model of growth, or a direction of growth, and it shows how a person doing this evolutionary work may direct her energies. For this, Sufi work owes a great deal to Islam, since Islam offers a model of practical life directed at *collectively harmonising individual and personal energies and commitments for an evolutionary purpose.*

---

2 Gold, E.J., *The Human Biological Machine as a Transformational Apparatus* (Gateways,'86)

Part–I

This is no place to stop—halfway between ape and angel.

Benjamin Disraeli
on evolution

Contemplation

Cease.

Let the tired, roving caravan

That's going nowhere, stop.

It's the time to become absent, become bereft

It's the time to receive the one who never left.

Clouds upon clouds of thoughts and sensations

Arise from the minds of numberless men

Filling the air like puffs of dust

Stricken, frightened humanity

Choking on its own polluted breath.

The world is a temple teeming with idols

So many gods, so many selves

So many idols for us to break

But, break as many idols as you may break

As long as you exist as a self

There is one more idol left to break.

(translated from Urdu)

Thoughts:
Meeting Points

In his first book, *The Tao Of Physics*, Fritjof Capra explored the meeting points between modern physics and mysticism. In *The Web Of Life* he has done a marvellous job of doing the same thing with biology and mysticism. What emerges in the process is a picture of life that is founded as much on the mind as it is on matter. This is not surprising if we remember that matter is not a fundamentally different reality from energy. It is more like a pattern of energy which, due to a particular design of our sense-perceptual system, assumes an unusual significance in our perceptual world. In his book, Capra has outlined the "systems view" of life and evolution, which brings matter and mind and energy and consciousness into a single, inherently indivisible framework.

From Capra's book we learn that the Darwinian/Neo Darwinian theories about random genetic change may not necessarily be the last word among biologists on the mechanism of evolution. On the basis of recent biochemical evidence it seems plausible that evolution may not be as passive a process as natural selection acting upon random genetic change makes it out to be. Theories concerning "symbiogenesis", or symbiotic participation of organisms in effecting genetic change are a serious alternative to Neo-Darwinian theories. Capra quotes Margulis and Sagan, "Life did not take over the globe by combat, but by networking."

Capra presents the late 20th century systems view according to which "the genome is seen as a self-organising network capable of spontaneously producing new forms of order." He quotes Stuart Kauffman, "Much of the order we see in organisms may be the direct result not of natural selection but of the natural order selection was privileged to act on. ......Evolution is not just tinkering......It is emergent order honoured and honed by selection."

Capra's exposition of Maturana and Varela's theory of cognition is illuminating in that this theory makes no distinction between living and cognition. "Cognition, then, is not a representation of an independently existing world, but rather a continual *bringing forth of a world* through the process of living" (emphasis in original). Capra writes further, "individual living systems are part of each other's worlds. They communicate with one another and co-ordinate their behaviour."

All this becomes directly relevant to some of the material in this book if it is recognised that there is a lot more going on around us than meets the eye. Capra himself says, "We all know that we see or hear phenomena only within a certain range of frequencies; we often do not notice things or events in the environment that do not concern us, and we also know that what we perceive is largely conditioned by our conceptual framework and our cultural context."

But if it is true that there is a whole lot more going on around us than we consciously perceive then it means that we live in an imperceptible as well as a perceptible world. It is also very likely that we ourselves are a lot more than we, or others around us, consciously perceive. Conscious perception is a highly selective device which natural selection has produced for a limited purpose. It enables organisms to navigate in a world of matter. But we have seen that what we actually live in is a world of energy. What appears to us as matter, with its solid feel or light reflecting substance, is our own sensory artifact. "Mind and world arise together," Capra quotes Varela as saying.

We are part of a continuum of energy and awareness, within which our existence as individual entities is a matter of definition and context. What we recognise as the spiritual impulse within us is the ongoing recovery of wholeness, which means that we apprehend at some level our larger existence, not as a part of the continuum but as the continuum itself. Interactions beyond the sensory realm with one another and the world become part of the field of awareness. These relationships also become immensely enjoyable. Our bodies do not, then, keep us apart.

From books like Capra's it is apparent that human attempts to understand the world and understand ourselves are finally coming of age as a single adventure. The great trap of matter and its illusions is being sprung open by scientists themselves—this time, not by physicists but by systems biologists. What a welcome surprise to find in the writings of Varela and co-authors the following lines: "This grasping after an inner ground is itself a moment in a larger pattern of grasping that includes our clinging to an outer ground in the form of the idea of a pregiven and independent world. In other words, our grasping after a ground, whether inner or outer, is the deep source of frustration and anxiety." It is no accident that we hear echoes of the Buddha. Separation of inner and outer is being seen by science for what it is—an artifact.

Non-Duality and Positive Duality

Overview: The enlightened person claims to be free of personal suffering. According to him this has been achieved through "realising" that the personal self is rooted in a lie. Is the personal self an *artifact* of the mind? Is there an evolutionary force in the human psyche to counter the hypnotic effect of this artifice—to see through it? Does the psyche, through the spiritual drive, seek a decisive end to suffering? Is "positive duality" a more practically achievable alternative to non-duality?

Am I in the world or the world in me?
Located in space or devoid of space?
May Thee rejoice in Thy spacelessness
*Pray tell me though, what is **my** place?*
(Quatrain by Iqbal, translated from Urdu)

Iqbal's question is well posed. Is this body all that we are? Are we also "spirit"? If so, where is the spirit *located*? Are we separate from one another or, at an imperceptible level, one?

In the Introduction I have mentioned the mystery of the non-dual consciousness which an "enlightened" individual is said to possess and enjoy. It is considered from different angles throughout the book, but it might be useful to highlight it here as it cuts right through the picture of the human being painted by science. The reality of the organism as a separate entity is, for good reasons, taken as self-evident in science. It is endorsed by normal experience. The fact of our existence as a body–localised and separated in space from other bodies and objects, is hardly open to question. We know that we exist because we recognise ourselves as a unique physical being. "I sense therefore I am" and I am because I sense myself. And this myself that I sense is a physical and chemical entity.

The mystery deepens however as this normal and natural dual consciousness begins to diminish in intensity and eventually vanish. In the experience of, and/or in the permanent transformation to, the so-called "self-realised" state, all trace of dual consciousness is lost. The person appears to spontaneously arrive at a "realisation" of the "quintessential unity of existence" which cannot possibly permit the existence of two.

But what does all this mean? I think the mistake often made by mystics and by writers on mysticism is that of elaborating on the issue as if it were a philosophical problem. What New Sufi thought attempts to do is to see it as a cognitive phenomenon. And to go further and speculate on a possible neurobiological basis for it. Even though the question of duality has great philosophical implications and may tend to engage our minds on that level, the attempt to solve it in philosophical terms is, I think, a virtual dead-end. On the other hand, posed as a quasi-scientific problem, it opens up enormous new areas of inquiry.

I believe that the new areas of theoretical and empirical inquiry provoked by the phenomenon of "enlightenment" are of great relevance to human existence. As we have seen, the "enlightened" or "self-realised" individual vehemently asserts that to achieve this state is to transcend fear and personal suffering and to dwell in a mental state of absolute fulfillment, joy and "freedom". It is a "liberated" state, claims the self-realised being—in which all confusion between absolute and relative is, once and for all, resolved. As such, New Sufi thought considers it reasonable to characterise self-realisation as a cognitive phenomenon and to assume that there is a neurological event or process, or set of processes, associated with it. With this as a working hypothesis, it becomes possible to ask further questions, and for this the general framework of evolutionary biology offers a fruitful starting-point. The questions are deep and fundamental. If duality is a cognitive phenomenon or a specific state of consciousness, what purpose does it serve? Conversely, what faculties and advantages are lost in non-dual consciousness?

We have seen that the organism is biased in its own favour. This self-bias, working in tandem with sense-supported establishment of a distinct chemical and physical identity, fuels the survival, as well as the procreative, drive. There is a strong, primal will to exist as a physical/chemical being. This is true of all forms of life. If self-bias were lost the biological drive to survive and procreate would be considerably weakened. The organism would be at a great disadvantage.

Only in isolated human beings is the phenomenon of non-dual consciousness manifested. One might presume that this extremely rare manifestation began a few thousand years ago as human consciousness was significantly relieved of the pressures of biological survival. The human brain began to develop entirely novel capacities. The earliest recorded evidence of the *systematic cultivation* of mystic experience is found in the *Vedas* of ancient India. It is most interesting that the human brain and human consciousness should be drawn at all to develop in a direction counter to self-bias and self-perpetuation. The phenomenon, though certainly exceptional, cannot be considered pathological. It tends to manifest in individuals with exceptionally well-developed cognitive and emotional capacities—individuals considered "wise" and worthy of respect.

Something apparently gives these rare and exceptional individuals in most cultures the impetus and invincible confidence to proclaim that the absolution of the human mind lies in the transcendence of self-bias. They proclaim the existence of a dynamic "evolutionary" force propelling individual human consciousness in this unusual direction.

There seems to me absolutely no way to fit this into the traditional evolutionary biology framework. It certainly cannot be considered an insignificant epiphenomenon. There is simply too much evidence that the "spiritual" impulse is of central value and relevance to human consciousness.

A major clue for New Sufi thought to piece together the puzzle comes from the strange fact that mystics invariably relate the transcendence of self-bias to the "dissolution of Maya"– insisting that the "personal self" is founded on a lie. Is this lie rooted in sensory illusion? Is perception of form an artifice of the mind? Is there an evolutionary drive in the human psyche to counter the hypnotic force of the artifice—to see through it? New Sufi thought pursues this line of inquiry and concludes that the pieces do indeed belong to the same picture and they seem to fit.

The enlightened being claims to be free of personal suffering. And this has been achieved, it seems to him or her, simply through a cognitive "shift".

The mystic may be forgiven for calling this shift as "waking up" and "seeing things as they really are". It would certainly appear that way to him. But surely something deep and basic has happened at the neurological level. There should be reason to suspect a fundamental change in neural connections, neural chemistry and neural programming.

Spiritual enlightenment is elusive. It plays hide and seek with the seeker—enticing him or her with fleeting glimpses of an evolutionary possibility. It seems to work in strange ways, according to unknown laws, or perhaps not subject to the rule of any law. How many of the large number of seekers so drawn actually succeed? What determines who will eventually make it?

I find it difficult to make sense of the experience of dramatic and spontaneous transformation without postulating the existence of an influence outside the human plane. I think the human nervous system is deeply linked to very subtle and very powerful forces existing outside the human plane. The feeling of being so connected, if and when it does become clearly perceptible, is awesome.

The mystery of non-duality and *positive duality* is resolved in this experience. The Source chooses how its influence shall be manifested. In non-duality the artificial reality of the personal self is seen through and attachment to it is dissolved. This produces an extraordinarily euphoric feeling of release. In positive duality connection with the Source takes the form of *reinforcing* personal identity but enabling individual consciousness to align with the will of the Source.

There are many well-known historical examples of each. The Buddha, Jesus, Shankaracharya, and numerous saints and mystics in all cultures, are examples of self-realised masters. Moses and Mohammed and many Sufi teachers are examples of individuals living in the state of positive duality, when one feels separate from God but deeply connected.

New Sufi thought postulates that the evolution of the primate-human brain toward a metaprimate level began several thousand years ago, as human beings became physically secure from the threat of predators and created settlements supported by large stocks of grains and other foods. Very gradually, scarcity-orientation, an inherited characteristic of the primate-human mind, began to change and the boundaries of human consciousness expanded beyond the universe of matter into a universe of energy. In this new universe, scarcity laws do not apply. It is the realm of the spirit. The realm of love.

We are a species in slow transition, struggling painfully to outgrow the fear and fright chemically etched in our primate brain and body. Having at our disposal weapons of awesome power, we are in a position to unwittingly bring doom to the world. Our brains remain rooted in an imagined sense of lack and scarcity. Can we outgrow this orientation and learn to tap the resources of the spirit where there is no such thing as scarcity?

Thoughts:
Non-Dual Consciousness and Accountability

Normal dual consciousness:
I act upon my will.
Positive dual consciousness:
I act upon Thy will.
Non-dual consciousness:
There is no will to act upon.

There is an interesting conversation between Swami Dayanand Saraswati and Andrew Cohen in the Fall/Winter 1998 issue of "What Is Enlightenment?" Swami Saraswati, a Gita scholar, decries the importance of enlightenment as an end-in-itself in isolation from the wholeness of spiritual growth. In the tradition of the Gita, he maintains that without the study and full understanding of the scriptures, *true* spiritual knowledge cannot be achieved. A genuine *jnani*, he says, also has complete mastery of the knowledge and due to this he is able to teach others. In Swamiji's scheme, the full cognitive power of self-understanding is obtained only through study under a scholar, disciplined living and right conduct, rather than a sudden "experience" of enlightenment. Although there are major differences between Swamiji's teachings and Sufi teachings and practices, both systems agree in their insistence on systematic transformation of the self through the conquest of indulgence.

Since we have very little understanding of the psychology of non-dual consciousness, the problem of accountability is immensely complicated. There is a powerful inner feeling that everything is happening by itself and that there is no free-will. As a result, there is no sense of accountability, since there is no "other".

In normal dual consciousness, as everyone knows, there is always an element of, at least apparent, personal decision. One is guided by one's sense of right and wrong, based on a variety of social, cultural and personal factors. One feels accountable to society, to the law of the land, to religion, to a personal code of ethics and morality and so on.

Positive duality appears to be an interesting mix of normal dual and non-dual consciousness. Here, the individual feels powerfully connected to a higher source of personal guidance. To this source, the person feels absolutely accountable. In most cases, guidance and instruction received from the source call for great personal sacrifice and self-control. Thus, a deep inner moral code seems to be in place which regulates not only behaviour but also thoughts and emotions. In time, this code of ethics is so deeply incorporated into one's feelings that one automatically acts according to it.

The great Urdu poet, Iqbal, has said in a marvellous couplet:
Make so high the level of thy own integrity
That, prior to each and every destiny,
May God inquire, what is **thy** *will?*

The new "rush" for enlightenment in Western society as an extreme form of self-indulgence fills one with dread. Would they invent someday a pill or a temporal lobe stimulator to produce enlightenment?

CHAPTER I

The Creation of Self

Overview: Is the concept of Maya scientifically meaningful? What do mystics mean when they say that the self is unreal? Is the self an artifact of the brain and the operating characteristics of sense perception? Is there, as the Buddha taught, no firm ground in reality? Is the human mind trapped in a world of artificial reality—a world of personal likes and dislikes and desires generated by Maya? Is liberation from Maya possible?

In the Indian mystical tradition one frequently comes across the term, Maya. It has a number of connotations, seemingly different, but actually closely related. One of these is the notion that the world, i.e., objects of perception, are "unreal". This doesn't make much sense to the Western mind and scientists typically dismiss it as mystifying and irrelevant to science. This is perhaps a typical example of the communication gap between two very sophisticated disciplines, with each one going about its worthy business without recourse to the other. I consider this as having rather serious and unfortunate consequences. Mystic insights are typically deep and intuitive. There is perhaps a certain unintended arrogance about them. They ring so deep in the mystic's mind as obvious, self-evident truths that no effort is made by the mystics themselves to investigate these "truths". This is not a very satisfactory situation. In this chapter I will try to bring scientific and mystic knowledge together on a series of questions pertaining to the biology and psychology of the mind (or brain) and its experience of the world.

Assume that you woke up one morning and found that your sense-perceptual apparatus had suddenly acquired the ability to receive inputs of energy of all possible frequencies and intensities without any filtering and without modulation. While you slept, some mysterious change had taken place in your brain and receptor chemistry, enabling photoreceptors in your eye to see over the complete (infinite) wavelength range, rather than the very narrow range of less than a micron (one millionth of a metre) of the normal human eye. Similarly, suppose that the peripheral sense receptors located in your skin tissue also were to suddenly become receptive to all possible energy signals in the environment.

It's a fair guess that you wouldn't perceive anything. The world for you would be a vast energy landscape, seamless and whole—a landscape of varying concentrations of energy, all connected together. It is unlikely that you would see or sense any "objects", or disconnected, distinct entities with clear boundaries.

You would also probably not be able to see or sense your own body in any way similar to the way you now do—a disconnected, distinct solid object with an unambiguous boundary.

It is hard to imagine what your sense of yourself, and of other selves, and the world would be like. Would you have a self at all? Would you see and sense yourself as "separate" from others—an entity that you can recognise and to which you can be absolutely committed?[1]

The mystic claims, without sufficient explanation, that our senses play an enormous hoax on us. He speaks in mystical terms to say this. But it can be shown that the claim is correct.

Evidence to this effect comes from biology, physics and psychology. First, from physics we learn about the nature of the electromagnetic spectrum of a radiating source, such as the sun. This curve, with intensity on the vertical axis and wavelength on the horizontal, looks like a hill, with a height that depends on the temperature of the source. The base is actually infinite, going from zero wavelength to infinity. But the height of the peak varies. In the case of the sun (**our** sun; there are many, many suns in the universe), the temperature is very high and the peak of the hill is very sharp and narrow, occupying a wavelength band of about 0.4 to about 0.7 microns. (Remember, a micron is one-millionth of a metre.) Well, now from biology, by studying the optical properties of the human eye and the sensing range of its photoreceptors, we find, not surprisingly, that the wavelength range of human vision matches almost exactly the tiny band of the solar radiation intensity peak. This is the band of visible light. The sun radiates over an infinitely large range, but the intensity of radiation falls off sharply outside the tiny peak band. Photoreceptors of the human eye are tuned to the solar wavelength band where the intensity is sharp and high. We are blind to other frequencies or wavelengths. (To the right of the tiny wavelength peak band is the range of infrared radiation, or heat. We do not see in this range, but our skin sense receptors feel the radiation as heat.)

Another important piece of the puzzle comes from the psychology of perception in the context of vision. Numerous experiments have been conducted to study visual perception, many of which indicate that perception necessarily involves a component of recognition. We don't simply see everything—we recognise things. For example, there are these picture books for children where you have to look for hidden objects in a drawing. Your success depends entirely on **recognition**. It might be too strong a statement to say that perception and recognition necessarily and invariably go together, but the existence of a strong correlation between them appears to be well established.[2]

Putting all these pieces together, some inferences can be drawn that are general and others perhaps that are not so general. From physics and the anatomy, physiology and operational characteristics of animal sensory systems, it is clear that sense perception is limited in numerous ways and by numerous parameters. And this is crucial in determining what we see and what we do not see (or sense). In turn, this determines what the world looks like to us. We see the world as a collection of solid objects, each with a distinct boundary. This way of seeing the world is an *artifact* of our visual sense perception system. To appreciate this point, imagine for a moment that our eyes could see molecules and atoms and particles smaller than atoms. The world, in such a case, would seem very different to us. We would see huge spaces between the particles within each solid object. There would be a lot more space than matter in each object. Since we would also be able to see the atoms and molecules of air surrounding the object, perhaps there would be no object to see in any familiar sense. It would all be one vast landscape of space and matter. And since matter, physics tells us, is nothing but energy packets, then the universe is undoubtedly one big seamless energy landscape of varying concentrations.

The conclusion to be drawn is the following. (And here we take account of the psychology of perception experiments as well). As organisms with a specific set of personal biases, we see and sense very selectively. In general, we are biologically programmed to look for and find what is of importance and interest. Our sense-perceptual system, like that of any other organism, has a functional basis. Most organisms have to worry about survival. They need to look for food and must be able to detect the presence of predators. Our sight, smell, hearing, etc., have evolved over several million years as aids to survival.

Human beings are organisms evolved from other animals. Our brains and bodies are basically designed the same way. But the ability to stand up straight and function from this stance has given our species unique abilities. Human cognitive development over the last ten or twenty thousand years has been so remarkable that it has created advantages, opportunities and problems which are uniquely human. The inner and outer landscape of human existence has many features common with other organisms and many that are absolutely different.

Let us return to our consideration of human sense perception. We see the world the way we do as a result of sense-perceptual selectivity and filtering. The mystic refers to this as distortion of consciousness. (Mystic thought does not articulate the detailed processes behind the distortion.) The chain of logic in New Sufi thought goes like this. The bias to exist as a chemically and physically unique entity predisposes and restricts consciousness. This shapes and influences the structure of the mind and the general texture of organic, including psychological, experience. (Some mystics make an emphatic distinction between awareness and consciousness. They refer to the former as impersonal and the latter as personal. Awareness is free, while consciousness is bound. In "liberation", consciousness is freed and becomes awareness.)

For organisms preoccupied with finding food and protection from predators this restriction of consciousness (or more correctly, awareness) is natural. For human beings it creates a very peculiar problem—something that has no place in the biological scheme. But to trace the complete spiral of evolution of consciousness, we need to start with the cell.

The cell has many outstanding features. One of these is its peripheral membrane, which is made up of two layers. The two layers are slightly separated and between them is an oily environment. The result is that many molecules, which prefer to bond with water rather than oil, cannot cross the membrane. The membrane is thus selectively permeable and this allows the internal environment of the cell to be, and remain, different from the external environment.

This is an example of *artifice*. The cell is preserving its physical and chemical identity. Actually, its real chemical identity is stored in the complex molecular pattern of the genes, which typically reside inside the cell's nucleus. The nucleus has its own enclosing membrane. Through a series of artifacts, the first assembled cell succeeded in separating itself, physically and chemically, from its surrounding lifeless environment and maintaining this separation. The cell apparently has a mysterious and fierce "investment" in preserving and perpetuating its genetic identity.

One of the many essential requirements for self-protection and self-replication to take place so ingeniously is for the cell's recognition system to be able to make out the cell's physical boundary **unambiguously**, i.e., to make an unambiguous distinction between self and not-self. For this, selective sensing is required[3]. We saw this on a larger scale by considering our own sense-perception system. If our senses perceived and saw *everything*, the boundary of our own body would be very ambiguous and perhaps its entire operation, biologically and psychologically, would be entirely different. We would certainly not be the sort of organisms we are (biologically and psychologically).

Due to the way our senses work, we see some things and do not see other things. As a result, we live in a patchy world—a collection of separate objects. Due to the way our senses are designed, we are predisposed to see dense concentrations of energy which reflect visible light and this light activates vision. We call these dense energy patches matter[4].

Our sense of touch also deludes us in somewhat the same way. Our body is a dense patch of energy. The molecules of our skin tissue have surface electrons, with a negative charge. These electrons form a negatively charged "cloud". Any solid object that we touch has a similar negative electron cloud at its surface. The two like-charged clouds repel each other when they come very close. This produces the signal in our sense receptors, which we call touch. As a result of this sensory mechanism, certain dense patches of energy which electrically repel our skin molecules and which reflect visible light, take on in our perceptual world a reality that seems to somehow stand out and appear special. This is our familiar material reality—a rather thin slice through the vast energy world we actually live in.

I will now do a hop, skip and jump and sketch out a scenario of development of increasingly complex artifacts as organisms evolved. The artifacts that life produces at the cellular level, as a result of the artifices it employs, may be called primary artifacts. The artifices are actually dazzlingly complex, as skimming a textbook of biochemistry would quickly show[5]. The immune system, for example, employs strategies and devices that are exceedingly ingenious and sophisticated. (This is human language, it means little in the natural world. The point simply is that the qualification, primary, in relation to strategies and artifacts at the microscopic or submicroscopic level of life does not mean they are any less complex than the series of artifacts we will be looking at presently, which we will designate 'secondary artifacts'.)

The process of biological evolution could perhaps be considered as a process of evolution of changing artifices employed by organisms in their struggle for survival. As multicellular organisms with billions of cells appeared on the scene, the artifices became layered into a hierarchy, from the very basic, instinct-type artifices employed by simple organisms, to complex higher-level " artifacts". Emotions are higher-level artifacts. Animals with endocrine glands have them. Emotions of fear, sexual urge and perhaps many others associated with glandular secretions may be considered secondary artifacts. Perhaps these are associated with rudimentary "thought" patterns. At this stage, probably, **conscious** strategising appeared. Many animals demonstrate a rudimentary ability to make conscious decisions, involving consideration of multiple alternatives. (Experiments on rats and monkeys are the best reported ones, but trained parrots also demonstrate remarkable decision-making skills.)

With this quick hop, skip and jump through the genealogy of life's artifacts, we come to Homo sapiens—a species with the largest repertoire of secondary artifacts. With the relatively rapid evolution of the neocortex and development of vocal chords, human speech and language developed quickly. The human mind became a factory of artifacts. The artifact of I-ness or selfevolved, along with the tendency to develop self-concepts.

It seems to me that the greatest complication (in the context of our analysis of human suffering) came about when the circuits of thought and emotion got inextricably coupled in the evolution of the human brain. One level of secondary artifact (thought) could now instantly influence body chemistry to a remarkable degree through the secretion of neuropeptides in the brain, as well as through endocrine glands. These chemicals have been appropriately called "molecules of emotion"[6].

From the "mystic" point of view, the upshot of these latest scientific discoveries is that the human mind functions primarily within the parameters of its own artifacts—thoughts and emotions, personal likes and dislikes, and hence in a kind of artificial reality. This artificial reality is filled with artifacts that are biologically and culturally programmed. The mind, working through the artifice of I-ness, identifies, conceptually and emotionally, with programmed notions which create personal likes and dislikes, leading to a further distortion of consciousness.

From the mystic's point of view the normal mind is constantly engaged in producing artifacts which appear to the mind as real. Some of these artifacts generate pleasant emotions and others unpleasant ones. It is all a game of primary and secondary artifacts. So, for the mystic, none of it has any "Reality", or rather it has only a relative reality, shaped by personal bias.

In mystic transformation something very extraordinary happens psychologically. Like the emperor's new clothes in the legendary story, the artifacts of mind lose their apparent reality. A shared hypnotic spell is broken. Consciousness is set free and personal suffering erased.

(In Chapter 6, The Human Being—Reconceived, I will discuss the Buddhist theory of the creation of self. According to the Buddha, all sense of constancy, including the constancy of self, is an illusion in that it is due to the mind's inability to perceive continuous change occuring at the core of physical reality. The illusion of self arises from the limitations of the mind. It is remarkable that with his Buddha eye, Gautama was able see into the heart of matter and perceive the transient and elusive nature of phenomena at the subatomic level.)

Notes:

1. In his book, A History Of The Mind (1), Nicholas Humphrey argues that the sense of "me" is fundamentally sense based. According to him, "me" and "my" go together. The following are quotes from his book: "On one side of the boundary lay 'me', on the other 'not-me': and it was 'my life', 'my form', 'my substance' that was at risk." "So boundaries—and the physical structures that constituted them, membranes, skins—were crucial. First, they held the animal's substance in, and the rest of the world out. Second, by virtue of being located at the animal's surface they formed a frontier: the frontier at which the outside world impacted the animal, and across which exchanges of matter and energy could take place."

   Somewhere along the line, Humphrey remarks cryptically that "unlike other bounded objects, such as a raindrop or a pebble or the moon, these [the organism's] boundaries are self-imposed and actively maintained." They are imposed and maintained by sensory feedback loops in which, according to his theory, incoming sensory signals are modulated by responsive feedback signals from the sensory cortex, and this what generates our sense of "me" as a bounded object.

   I think Humprey is right to insist on the use of "me" in place of "I", which

---

1 Humphrey, N., A History of the Mind (Simon & Schuster, 1992).

is an inherently nebulous notion. "Me" makes it sensory and physical and thus cognitively specific. I think the discussion of duality would be better carried out by phrasing it as me-thou, rather than I-thou. This is an interesting insight because when he talks about "my form", "my substance" etc., he is also putting his finger on the kernel of psychological change that occurs in enlightenment. The mind no longer identifies the body as "my" form or "my" substance. It is almost as if, psychologically, all sense of boundedness is given up. The sense of "me" is no longer based on matter and its physical and chemical identity. (Throughout the book I have maintained that perception of matter is a sensory artifact. If we could see gaseous molecules or radiation other than visible light, or consciously sense over a much wider range of tactile signals, our sense of the physical world, and "our" bodies and other bodies would be vastly different. I therefore agree with Humphrey that the organism's boundaries are self-imposed and actively maintained. But my way of looking at the matter is a bit different.)

2. It is well-established that sensory channels in animals function like electrical data transmission channels, with upper and lower thresholds and various other characteristics. A good source of information on the neuroanatomy and physiology of vision is Francis Crick's *The Astonishing Hypothesis*(2). Modulation characteristics of sensory channels and perception, especially vision, are not well understood. But there are many speculative models. Karl Pibram's early work, reported in "The Neurosciences" (M.I.T. Press,1974), is an example.There is little question that sense-perception is a means to an end—survival of the organism. But the exact nature of its limitations in different species and modulation of signals is not known. Obviously, signals are modulated and processed according to some program, creating coherent images. Are these true images of the world? Larry Dossey, in his book, *Space, Time And Medicine*,(3) refers to a remarkable anecdote supposedly reported by Darwin. Dossey writes, "His ship, The Beagle, after anchoring off the Patagonian coast, dispatched a landing party in small rowboats. Amazingly, the Patagonian natives watching from the shore were blind to The Beagle, but could easily see the tiny rowboats! They had no prior experience of monstrous sailing ships, but canoes—small rowing vessels, were an everyday part of their life." (I could not find this anecdote in *The Voyage Of The Beagle*.) Crick's book also has a good chapter on the psychology of visual perception—a fair amount of experimental information, combined with speculation on how the brain actually "sees". Also of interest and fun to read is the chapter, To See And Not See, in Oliver Sacks' *An Anthropologist On Mars*.(4)

---

2   Crick, Francis, *The Astonishing Hypothesis*. (Touchstone,1994).
3   Dossey, L., *Space, Time And Medicine*. (Shambhala,1982).
4   Sacks,O., *An Anthropologist on Mars*. (Picador,1995).

3. As far as I know, despite the enormous amount of research on the cell, its "sensory system" has yet to be adequately modeled. How does the cell's pattern recognition system work? Where is the processing done? How does the cell "know itself" (assuming that's a scientifically meaningful question)? What signal screening and filtering mechanisms, if any, are involved to facilitate the process of self-recognition? How are signals converted to data? How does the cell "perceive"? Does it have a "psychology" of perception (either similar or dissimilar to our own)? I suspect that some form of predisposition or bias is required even at the cellular level to perceive things. If everything could be seen, meaning all signals in the universe received, I doubt that anything would be seen or made sense of. Incidentally, a somewhat similar conundrum exists in thermodynamics and information theory concerning anthropomorphism and entropy (see, for example, "Is Entropy An Anthropomorphism?" in *Modern Developments In Thermodynamics*, B. Gal-Or, ed.)(5)

4. The equivalence of mass and energy is widely known, thanks to Einstein's simple equation. But it is quantum mechanics that has forever altered our view of matter. With everything interpreted in terms of energy and forces and waves and probabilities, the concept of materiality and its specialness to commonsense and sense-perception, crumbles before our eyes.

5. A few examples of artifices employed by "life" at the molecular level are described in readable detail by Michael Behe in his book, *Darwin's Black Box*.(6) He argues that these are so complex and involve so many intermediate steps with no survival value attributable to the intermediate steps that the hypothesis of random mutations and natural selection as the sole agents of evolutionary change is untenable. It seems to me, as an outsider, that the debate is at least partly philosophical and metaphysical. Unlike experiments in physics and chemistry, evolutionary processes cannot be tested in the laboratory. If it ever becomes possible to synthesise life in the laboratory and it is observed that basic organic molecules can spontaneously arrange themselves to produce elementary properties of life, it would be a first step toward real scientific confirmation. But at least some of the intermediate steps at the molecular level would also have to be observed as occurring by themselves. Until then, Behe's case seems fairly strong, even though I find his speculations about the possible origin, or source "behind" the molecular artifacts of life, quite arbitrary. The scientific strength of his case lies in its identification of deep questions which current evolutionary theory tends to leap over in huge leaps of faith. Fritjof Capra (1997) presents in outline Lynn Margulis' theory of symbiogenesis, which is quite strikingly at odds with many Darwinian ideas and attempts to fill many gaps. Capra's explanation of "autopoiesis" is also excellent.

---

5 Gal-Or, B., ed., *Modern Developments In Thermodynamics*. (Academic Press, 1973).
6 Behe, M., *Darwin's Black Box*. (Touchstone.1998).

6. In an old, but fascinating book, *Man's Presumptuous Brain*, A.T.W. Simeons(7) discusses the link between mind and body, with special reference to psychosomatic illnesses, using the structure and anatomical evolution of the human brain as backdrop. Some of his analysis is speculative, but it is relevant to the evolution of what I have called, higher-order secondary artifacts in human beings in a precise clinical and etiological sense. For information on the role of neuropeptides, see Pert,C., *Molecules Of Emotion*.(8)

7 Simeons, A.T.W., *Man's Presumptuous Brain*. (Dutton,1962).
8 Pert, Candace, *Molecules of Emotion*. (Scribner,1997).

Thoughts:
A Sufi Joke

As one would expect, a Sufi joke is no ordinary joke. Here's an example.

Three blind persons and a person with sight stood next to an elephant. Each of the three blind persons felt a part of the elephant—the trunk, a leg and the sides, and said it was a rope, a pillar and a wall. The one who could see laughed. "Little do you know what you are touching," he said mockingly. "This is an elephant. I know what an elephant is because I can see it. It is black and very big. Its skin is thick and its trunk long. It weighs more than half a ton. That is an elephant." And he turned towards the elephant for confirmation.
The elephant looked quietly at the man. Then it presented its rear end and let out a gust of wind.

Who are the three blind persons and the person with sight? Who is the elephant?

It is easy to make all this a subject of learned discourse and scholars and students of Sufism may do so. But if you asked a Sufi teacher what the story is really about the likely answer would be, "elephant's fart."

CHAPTER II

The Evolutionary Impulse

Overview: Is there something fundamentally missing in the present science of biology? Is there a direction of growth inherent in the evolution of consciousness? Can this be identified? Does the human mind grow naturally in the direction of transcendence of bias?

Earlier I spoke obliquely of the existence of a unique "evolutionary impulse" in human beings. I suggested that there is a drive in the human psyche to break through the delusion produced by the mind's creation of artifacts.

A speculative sketch of how and why the mind creates artifacts was given in Chapter 1.

Several things stand out in the analysis, and I will mention them briefly here. We saw (or speculated on) how the "delusion" originates in the existence and organisation of the cell. The cell literally conceives itself as a separate entity, i.e., manufactures its separateness through a series of complicated artifices. Science (biochemistry) has never tried to see the cell's organisation in this "mystic" light. There is no adequate scientific model for the filtering and processing algorithms required for the cell to recognise itself—its physical and chemical territory—as a prerequisite to protecting its identity. The point I was trying to make is that this identity is a manufactured one—it is an artifact.

In complex, multicellular organisms, such as ourselves, sensory filtering is well understood, as we saw in the instance of vision in Chapter 1. To a great extent, but not completely, the illusion of separateness is created by the senses*. The organism's mind is charged with the responsibility of guarding the specific territory containing the set of genetically unique cells that physically make up the individual. Thus it is imperative that the boundary of this territory (the organism's body) be unambiguously

---

* (see Note #1, Chapter 1)

established. Sensory filtering and the algorithms in the brain concerned with perception are designed to accomplish this.

But we also saw that we actually live in a sea of energy—a vast, seamless, unbroken landscape, broken up into separate, disconnected objects by our sense-perception. We ourselves (our bodies) are simply "patches" and specific patterns of energy within this vast energy landscape.

However, we see and sense everything from within, rather than from outside ourselves. So we cannot see and sense ourselves as described above. Due to deep biological programming we are powerfully vested in the illusion of separateness and something truly extraordinary must happen to break this biological spell and bring about liberation. This is the reason mystic experience, and permanent mystic transformation, is so exceptional. It zaps and alters, momentarily or permanently, the organism's vested interest in separateness. The illusion is cleared up and "Reality" is revealed—a term used in mystic and Sufi literature as a counterpoint to illusion. (The precise Arabic terms used in Sufism are better translated as the real and the apparent, implying that the real is not the same as the apparent and lies "behind" it—hence, the expression, lifting the veil.)

Another term that the mystic uses to describe this illusion is distortion of awareness. The deeply ingrained biological investment in separation causes a whole chain of distortions which become the cause of conflict and suffering in the world.

(Sometimes in mystical teachings an interesting distinction is made between awareness and consciousness. Awareness is used to indicate a state of unbiased perception, whereas consciousness is always personally biased.)

According to the hypothesis of the evolutionary impulse, something in the human psyche pushes against the fundamental distortion of awareness. There is an evolutionary force working behind the scene to release awareness from vested interest in a particular body and mind—which means, release from identification with a body and its I.

The degree to which this evolutionary force is "felt" by the mind varies from total unresponsiveness to its presence to acute awareness of the pressure created by its subtle demand for acknowledgment and expression. As a result, we have, on the one hand, an overwhelming mass of humanity with very little conscious feeling of this internal pressure and, on the other, the *potential* mystic, who experiences unbearable stress due to the pressure. (The mystic is one within whose consciousness this evolutionary force has reached its natural point of fulfillment.)

Most cultures of the past were sensitive to the reality of this hidden dynamic within the individual psyche (they would have termed it, the individual "soul"). Their literature and their scriptures acknowledged it in subtle, indirect terms, using metaphors and symbols alien to our minds, just as the rather explicit way we are looking at the dynamic here would be alien to their thinking. But the important point is that in some form or another it was acknowledged and understood as a form of evolution. The "enlightened" person was invariably looked upon with awe and deep respect.

But we live in the age of science and science only accepts things it understands using its own method. This method constrains it to accept as valid empirical data, only sensory data which is standardised and common to everyone's experience. As a result, a very large, and personally very meaningful, part of human experience is excluded from scientific consideration. Due to the limitations of its method, science's understanding of the human being is narrow and relatively crude.

There would be no great harm in this, if this fact were to be clearly seen by science and a candid admission made to that effect. Unfortunately, modern biology—the way it is presented and taught and used, e.g. as the foundation of medical theory and practice, communicates a specific, precisely formulated picture of the human being, with the implicit assertion that this picture is basically sound and reasonably complete, except for further *details* which would be progressively filled in by ongoing scientific work.

Biologists are likely to make out the case that scientific instruments have extended, far beyond the realm of direct sensory perception, the range of data on which their picture and understanding of the human organism is based. Scientists are now able to track even intricate molecular processes of the body. The conventional mood and thinking in contemporary science is thus very upbeat—it is taken for granted that an increasingly refined and complete understanding of not only the human body, but also the human brain, is being firmly brought within the grasp of science[1].

What is not recognised is that scientists looking through their sophisticated instruments see only what the instruments are designed to look for in accordance with the established, a priori assumptions that make up the total paradigm of modern biology. And it is not only the design of instruments in accordance with a guiding paradigm that limits the scope of observation but also, more dramatically, the design of the perceptual apparatus of the experimental investigator! This apparatus exists within the investigator's brain. This too is an instrument—a system that has been designed over millions of years by exigencies of survival in specific environmental niches and specific environmental conditions, as we saw in Chapter 1. It has its own biases, design characteristics and design limitations. Experiments in the psychology of perception lend credence to the idea that we see things according to pre-set rules that are genetically and culturally programmed.*

Thus, if one were to entertain the possibility that the guiding paradigm in biology is fundamentally incomplete, then many of its theoretical and experimental models become suspect, and may even begin to seem naïve. Biologists study the human organism in intricate detail, modeling and tracking its internal biochemical processes. The periphery of the body is assumed to define the boundary of the system. This appears to accord with commonsense and normal sensory experience. It is assumed that each organism, confined within the visually observed periphery of the body, is the system to be studied and its interactions with the environment tracked. On this view, all organisms are closed systems, interacting with each other through speech, sight, smell, touch and hearing.

---

* (see Note #2, Chapter 1)

What if this view is fundamentally erroneous?

We have already seen that our senses deceive us. They are components of an essentially biased system. Physics tells us that what appears to us as a material body is a configuration of energy that is inextricably embedded in a vast and seamless energy landscape. Our senses, or rather, our sense-perceptual system, is designed to perceive very selectively. We do not perceive the continuous, interconnecting landscape, but only certain energy patches in it which meet our sensory design limitations. On account of biological and cultural biases, our minds perceive our bodies as disconnected, distinct, bounded material entities. Our minds are programmed to believe in this well-crafted sensory illusion and be absolutely committed to protecting the body as a separate entity. It is the hoax on which biological life is founded. It has fueled biological evolution on this planet over a period of four billion years.

The personal evolutionary hypothesis central to New Sufi thought must be considered against this backdrop. This hypothesis superimposes another kind of evolution on the ground-structure of biological evolution. This new evolution is characteristically human (advanced Homo sapiens) and individual. I suspect that it has a physical, probably neurological and biochemical, correlate in the brain. I believe that the "hoax" is biologically programmed in the operations of the brain and would have to be undone there, in the case of a genuine mystic transformation.

Throughout written historical records, a period of at least six or seven thousand years, one finds references to mystic experience. The impression one gets from these is that mystic experience (and lasting mystic transformation) is a well established fact, but also something that is extremely rare and treasured as exceptionally precious. Expositions of the phenomenon are found in ancient Hindu scriptures and an entire philosophical system of "spiritual" evolution is conceived around it. Certain extraordinary texts, such as Patanjali's *Yoga Sutras*, are practice manuals for spiritual evolution. So also are the pristine teachings of Buddhism.

The extreme rarity of mystic experience and mystic transformation would normally be considered feeble evidence for the possibility of an evolutionary force working within the human psyche in a subterranean fashion in opposition to the instinct of self-preservation. But the case for the kind of evolutionary force we are considering here rests not so much on conventional empirical evidence, but its opposite! People who are troubled by an unnamed and unnameable distress—sometimes referred to vaguely as spiritual seeking, find themselves helplessly and compulsively driven in the direction of mystic transformation. The seeking becomes increasingly troubled and restless, completely at odds with conventional notions of emotional illness, and is progressively and decisively consummated as attachment to self and its importance is given up.

New Sufi thought hypothesises that this "drive" is a natural driving force in the psyche towards the undoing of the illusion of personal separateness.

We have seen that from the point of view of physics an individual human body is a specific configuration of energy inextricably embedded in a continuous energy landscape. One of the propositions of New Sufi thought is that within this energy web, each individual body is intimately connected with other bodies in ways not consciously registered by the mind. For perfectly good reasons, some of which we have discussed, the mind, or consciousness, is configured to not register the connectedness. A clear, unambiguous sensory boundary must be established artificially to support the illusion of separation.

The proposition is that some part of the psyche—a *subliminal* form of consciousness, possesses awareness of the background energy landscape and the underlying connectedness of individual bodies below the level of normal consciousness. This results in a subtle condition of tension between different elements of perception—one, sensory, and the other, *episensory*.

The spiritual quest is a natural response of the mind to break the illusion of separateness.

———————————————

Notes:

1. Some scientists believe that it is, in principle, possible for science, by using its characteristic method, to arrive at a complete understanding of everything, including the human being. This position is based on a number of assumptions. With respect to the human being, for example, it is assumed that an increasingly complete and encompassing model can be incrementally arrived at by studying the brain and the body with more and more precision and theoretical and experimental ingenuity. It is believed that neurobiology will eventually tell us everything about every conceivable brain state in terms of neural firing patterns and neurotransmitters (see, for example, Wilson, E.O., *Consilience—the Unity of Knowledge*)(1). And this, in conjunction with genetic mapping and molecular biology and sophisticated models of brain-body interaction will yield a more and more complete understanding of the human organism— its states of consciousness, feelings, emotions, thoughts and behaviour. Various objections to this position can be raised in light of the analysis we are conducting in this book, using mystic insights and some fairly straightforward physics, psychology and biology. The human organism, or any organism, is not a closed system which can be studied, let alone understood, by examining its "hardware". It is a quintessentially nebulous system, with an undefined boundary, inextricably embedded in a larger, practically open-ended, energy landscape. How the human body and brain are affected and influenced by this infinite environment can never be modelled in absolute terms, simply because the infinite environment is made up of not only sensory, but also episensory and suprasensory realms, which are, by definition, unmodelable. As we shall see, the presence of these other realms is suggested by a huge mass of evidence, along with strong indications that the laws of physics characteristic of our normal realm of experiential reality do not apply to those realms. Since experiments cannot be conducted in those other realms, they are unmodelable. It is naïve to try to reduce the human being to the hardware of body and brain. The human organism is a "soft" system, inextricably embedded in a "soft" world (see, for example, Capra, Fritjof, *The Web of Life*) (2).

---

1 Wilson, E.O., *Consilience—The Unity of Knowledge*. (A.A. Knopf, 1998).
2 Capra, F., *The Web of Life* (Harper Collins, 1997).

CHAPTER III

Spirituality and Self-Unconcern

In the Introduction a drive antithetical to Self-Concern was mentioned and was designated as Self-Unconcern. This postulate will be discussed in detail in Chapter 6. It is this drive which finds expression in what is called spirituality.

The spiritual quest is a movement away from the personal. It is an evolutionary movement and it fits in very well with the hypothesis of the evolutionary impulse (Chapter 2). Its thrust is to set the personal consciousness free and allow it to merge with the suprapersonal. In the words of Nisargadatta, the great Advaita teacher, liberation is never of the person, it is always from the person. Everything that is personal is expressed through the Self-Concern drive. Usually this drive creates its own personal universe within the psyche—a cluster of personal artifacts, collectively designated in Chapter 6 as the Self-Concern System.

The two drives, Self-Concern and Self-Unconcern, compete for attention and expression in human consciousness. Since Self-Concern is the dominant mode, Self-Unconcern has to insinuate itself into our lives to claim its due by passive and active means. Sleep is a passive form of Self-Unconcern. Meditation is an expressive form.

Throughout history, cultures have made allowances for the Self-Unconcern drive. Its force and needs were acknowledged, usually under the label of spirituality. Mundane and supramundane were considered as two dimensions of human life. Spiritual teachers were honoured and valued. There was always a tacit acknowledgment of the spiritual dimension and its relevance, despite the fact that it is hidden from view and commonsense.

One of the most serious forms of damage caused by Western science to the wholeness of life has been the implicit devalidation of the spiritual dimension. Part of the blame for this must go to traditional concepts of spirituality, which were centred round an invisible and undefinable something, called the spirit. Spirit was actually considered to exist in some nonphysical form and various imaginative cosmologies were created around this concept. Since there was no evidence for the existence of spirit, the validity of the spiritual element of human consciousness came to be rejected in the West—more implicitly than explicitly.

Postulation of the Self-Unconcern drive does not hinge in any way on the existence of spirit as an entity. Rather, this drive, along with Self-Concern, is assumed to be part of the dynamic of the psyche. The personal and the suprapersonal coexist within the psyche as thesis and antithesis. They compete for attention and expression and the function of a healthy ego is to create a dynamic equilibrium or synthesis. For the majority of human beings, the balancing of these two opposite pulls takes place unconsciously. If they are not properly balanced, the result is a particular form of psychic distress.

As a human being grows spiritually, the point of balance shifts towards the suprapersonal. It manifests typically as spiritual seeking—a vague sense of incompleteness, seeking fulfillment and closure. Enlightenment is the point of absolute closure. It is a state of absolute suprapersonalness. In this state all identification with the personal is withdrawn.

Unfortunately, enlightenment is a happenstance. It cannot be made to happen. The best one can do is to prepare the mind and believe in the adage, chance favours the prepared mind. For some strange reason, the probability of enlightenment seems to be much higher in the company of an enlightened person.

Contemporary culture and its institutions have no understanding of the Self-Unconcern drive. Our world now is largely economically driven. Its entire metaphysical basis is involvement with the personal. There is no place in it for the Self-Unconcern drive. But, since it is a basic drive, its needs cannot be denied, regardless of whether they are acknowledged or not. It insinuates itself into our lives in various modified forms—mostly as distress created by over-emphasis of the personal self. Large numbers of people are turning to meditation and spiritual practice to satisfy the needs of the Self-Unconcern drive, seeking relief and refuge from the pettiness of the personal.

I believe there is a way around the peculiar problem of enlightenment—the problem being the fact that absolute closure of the Self-Unconcern drive is to be found in enlightenment and that enlightenment cannot be made to happen. The solution is to progressively reduce one's involvement with the personal. This need not always take the form of spirituality. Even relationships which transcend the personal can satisfy the needs of the Self-Unconcern drive.

This framework takes part of the mystery out of spirituality. It shows that spirituality is not a form of involvement with the self, but a form of non-involvement. Spiritual growth may be measured by this yardstick.

————————————

Thoughts:
Neurology and Self-realisation

V.S. Ramachandran, a distinguished neuroscientist, has predicted that the first half of the next century would be known in the history of science as the decades of neurology and mind-body medicine. Would all aspects of the mind be reduced eventually to physical processes of the brain? It would require progressively more sophisticated empirical techniques to track down the extremely complex neural activity underlying psychological processes and it might be a while before testable theories and models are developed. But the trend is absolutely clear. Already, a great deal has been discovered about precise areas of the brain where various activities are located. In the book, *Phantoms In The Brain*, Ramachandran himself has decisively crossed the traditional lines separating medicine from psychology and psychology from philosophy. He has presented fascinating theories on consciousness, identity, free will and mystical experience.

As I have said earlier, I believe the crucial missing piece of clinical data is the phenomenon of self-realisation. I believe its significance is fundamental because it sabotages the me—thou dichotomy that is so natural to life. Why should self-realisation—a psychological phenomenon in which this dichotomy is eroded in a significant way, result in a wonderful "lightness of being", freedom from anxiety, worry and fear, a profound release of natural affection for all human beings, absence of automatic reflexes in defence of the psychological self, and so on? By all accounts, self-realisation is a highly enjoyable transformation, so much so that it is the goal of many (but not all) religions. What is it in the psyches of individuals drawn to spiritual seeking that responds to this call to transcend me-thou dichotomy? Does the psyche possess some latent knowledge of a state beyond this dichotomy?

But first we need a better understanding of the dichotomy. Every organism is naturally biased in its own favour. There is a powerful sense of identification with the body and the many manifestations of the self in human beings. The brain constantly strategises to seek satisfaction of the needs of the body and the psychological self (or selves). How does spirituality fit into this scheme? What psychological mechanism is involved in the psyche's transcending of the body and the self?

The primate-human mind is the natural mind. It is designed to place its own embodied and psychological self first in order to propagate the individual's genes effectively. On this foundation it builds its circle of affection, restricting it to family, friends, race, tribe, etc., and shutting out individuals and groups considered as "others"—competitors, potential threats and so on.

In human beings spiritual growth happens spontaneously and naturally. And in that process the mind's self-bias begins to weaken. A marvellous awareness develops that "one is not this body and its mind"—in fact, not this organism. The mind begins to evolve into a metaprimate mind. As we shall see this automatically changes one's relationship to matter. The metaprimate mind sees matter as an artifact, not a pre-given reality. Hence the separateness that goes with matter begins to evaporate.

Can science help us understand the nature of spirituality without wittingly or unwittingly demeaning it? It would take a lot more than neurology to do this. And even a lot more than psychology, as we know it now. It cannot be done without including in some way the human organism's relationship with the imperceptible. Science would have to acknowledge the data which points to this. As matters now stand, such data are simply ignored since they do not fit into the picture. The logic seems to be: Oh, it must have a natural explanation since everything has a natural explanation. Philosophically yes, but why assume that human-made scientific instruments, now or at any particular time in the future, have or would have the ability to make perceptible *everything* significant?

CHAPTER IV

The "I" and its Apparent Disassembly

Overview: Is it possible to explain the sense of "I" in neuropsychological terms? If so, can self-realisation also be so understood? What is its psychological fallout? Can self-realisation be "induced"? In this chapter and the next I mention and discuss some anecdotal accounts of enlightenment in an attempt to pierce the mystery of the "I" and its apparent disassembly.

The sages of the past, dating as far back as the *Vedas*, reveal in their teachings and writings an uncanny intuitive grasp of the operations of the human mind or at least certain crucial aspects of it. They knew nothing about the brain in biomedical terms, nothing about the physics and biology of sense perception, or about the evolutionary history of the human brain and body. Yet they seem to have understood at some level the role of the brain in "constructing reality" and the brain's normal reactions to incoming stimuli *based on this construction*.

Obviously their theories of *maya, samsara,* duality, etc. were founded on "self-data", in other words deep personal experience of states of the mind in which this normal construction and normal responses are replaced by something startlingly different. These other states of mind led them to the "knowledge" that the "separate self" is an artifact. It is in some unknown manner assembled by the mind, resulting in the experience of duality. In genuine enlightenment this artifact is undone. In the words of the great classical Urdu poet, Ghalib:

> *Deft though we are in breaking all idols*
> *As long as WE are there's one more idol to break*
> (translated from Urdu)

Thus, in some mysterious way these sages had access to some extraordinary knowledge, founded on deep personal experience of an extraordinary set of altered *states*. Enlightenment, however, is not an altered *state*. It is a permanent transformation of perception, understanding and responses to events, startlingly different from the syndrome of experiences and responses associated with the normal sense of a separate "I" and its need to protect and preserve itself.

I am concerned with several related questions in this chapter, and throughout the book. How does the artifact of the "I" arise? How is the artifact undone in enlightenment? What are the implications and consequences of the presence and absence of this artifact? The questions are so fundamental that they cannot be answered by science at present. They can best be discussed under the umbrella of an emerging, new discipline, indicated by some writers as neurophilosophy[1]. The role of neurophilosophy is to bridge the gap between the "hard" neurosciences and "soft" sciences, such as psychology of perception, psychology of consciousness, etc.

So far, I believe that even the most gifted scientists, psychologists and philosophers working in this area are unaware of the possibility of a missing centrepiece to this great puzzle. Namely, the possibility that the so-called "I", or "I-ness", is a neurobiological artifact and that, secondarily, it is a syndrome of several identifiable neuropsychological processes. Once this possibility is admitted into the framework of serious inquiry, a great many related questions, e.g. those concerning enlightenment, fall into place and can be seen as part of a single large picture. *This picture, I believe, is the key to future human destiny.*

To begin to unravel the mystery of "I-ness", let us first look at some anecdotal accounts of enlightenment. Individuals who claim to have undergone the psychological transformation, labelled as enlightenment, "self realisation", or simply "realisation", testify to an extraordinary change in perception, experience and reactions to events. But there is a serious problem here. The terms enlightenment, realisation, etc, are poorly defined, if defined at all. Is there just one kind of enlightenment or many different kinds? The term itself is a deep verbal embarrassment. It has an aura of awe and blocks many serious questions which ought to be asked. By rolling so much into one word we create not mystery but mystification. Since there are no *external* indicators of the experience, or rather the transformation, it is all but impossible to study it. First-hand accounts of these altered psychological states are the only "evidence" one may go by. By its very nature this evidence, although extremely intriguing and valuable, is difficult to make much sense of in our own normal frame of experience. Some of the ensuing mystification is thus unavoidable, like trying to describe sweetness to someone who has no taste-buds. On the other hand, by not making crucial distinctions and trying to discriminate between different types of so-called enlightenment experiences, we end up deepening our ignorance.

It appears to me that there are major differences, as well as significant overlap, between such experiences. The person's sense of I-ness is undoubtedly deeply altered. But, as we know, this may also happen in numerous instances of chemical or physical changes in the brain due to damage and/or biochemical imbalances. Many neuroscientists have presented cases in popular books which sound like instances of deep spiritual experiences, e.g. V.S. Ramachandran, Oliver Sacks and Francis Crick (see Bibliography). Patients may describe a great sense of euphoria, peace, "letting go of the personal Self", and even the feeling of "suddenly understanding *everything*". Ramachandran believes that in most such cases physical or chemical changes in the temporal lobes of the brain are involved. Of course, it is well known that some such experiences can be temporarily induced through psychotropic drugs.

Let us consider the statements of Ramesh Balsekar, a contemporary enlightened master. Very much in line with the famous Advaita philosophy of India, Balsekar disclaims having any sense of free will. He vehemently maintains that free will is an illusion and implies that the phenomenon of enlightenment corresponds to the dispelling of this illusion harboured by the brain. There is a "sudden shift of perspective", whereby the conscious psychological operations of the brain are perceived without any sense of personal "involvement".

A fascinating interview with Balsekar appears in the American journal, "What Is Enlightenment?", Fall/Winter 1998, and is entitled, "Close Encounters of the Advaita Kind: The Euphoric Nihilism" of Ramesh Balsekar (see Bibliography). Balsekar is an acclaimed "Jnani"- a realised person belonging to the Advaita tradition, who "came to a sudden *final understanding*" while he was translating for Nisargadatta Maharaj, one of the most well known Advaita teachers of the second half of this century. What was the sudden "final understanding"? Balsekar quotes the Buddha: Events happen, deeds are done, there is no individual doer thereof. As the title of the article implies, the nihilism of this "final understanding" is euphoric.

In his book, *The Astonishing Hypothesis*, Francis Crick has dealt with the question of free will from a neurobiological point of view. He has speculated not only on the neural mechanisms involved in the mind's psychological "sense" of free will, but also the precise location within the brain where the feeling of free will arises. He cites some medical data to support his "astonishing hypothesis" that free will is a feeling which is a product of a set of physical processes in the brain. He mentions the case of a woman who "lost her sense of free will", following damage to a particular region of the brain. On recovering from the brain damage she was able to describe what it felt like to have been in that condition. She had been able to follow conversations but had not talked because "she had nothing to say". Her mind had been "empty" and she felt at peace. (In his book, *Phantoms In The Brain*, V.S. Ramachandran also writes about several cases involving striking distortions of neural structures implicated in the mechanism of free will.)

A sense of non-doership is very common among mystics. It is described in various ways. One mystic would say things like, " I see myself talking, responding, doing things, etc." Another one might say that they feel themselves being spontaneously moved by energy or "spirit" in everything "they" do, so that they disclaim not only doership but also their own existence! This may be called the "spectator syndrome"[2].

Is there, then, any difference between these persons and the patients described by the above medical scientists? What might have happened within the Buddha's brain in the moment of his enlightenment? How is the Buddha's enlightenment different from, say Balsekar's or some other such Guru's, assuming that it is? There are many cases of so-called enlightenment reported by persons whose credentials in other areas, e.g. basic morality, are suspect.

Let me hazard a guess about the Buddha. I believe he had an extraordinarily keen intelligence, combined with an extraordinary will and an equally extraordinary desire to "*experience reality first-hand*". He gave himself to the pursuit— body, mind and soul, peeling one layer of "artifact" after another and delving deeper and deeper into the mind. But how does one *know* what is real and what is artifact? You can, if you have the "Buddha mind"—if you are either blessed with it or devote yourself to developing it (see Chapter 5). The Buddha-mind enables you to tell the real from the artificial simply from the "taste" of the experience. The artificial may cleverly deceive but is eventually found out. Its taste fades, it rings hollow, it leaves a residue which disturbs, rather than fulfills, the soul. Like sea water, it increases rather than quenches our thirst. It all depends on whether we have the inclination to experience reality first-hand. If the inclination is strong enough it will take us there.

So in enlightenment something happens to the brain to *shock* it into a recognition of the real. Hence the term, realisation. But, beware! There is a trap. Not all "enlightenment" is necessarily real, just as all that glitters is not gold! The brain's circuitry can be literally shocked into a different neural arrangement by a power bolt from outside, e.g. into an arrangement where the sense of personal free will no longer exists. Such "power bolts" usually happen to a few rare individuals in the presence of some enlightened teachers who seem to command such exceptional power, or perhaps these teachers themselves are no more than participants in the process.

There is an eminent spiritual tradition in India called Kashmir Shaivism, in which it is assumed that the disciple receives enlightenment not only *through* the Guru's grace but also *from* the Guru—by a look, or a touch or even thought. To some extent, this belief is fairly prevalent in India in various forms. Hence the central significance of personal association with the Guru and absolute submission to him. One of the most outstanding popularisers of this teaching and practice in the West are Swami Muktananda and his successor, Swami Chidvilasananda. Swami Muktananda was a powerful Yogi and conducted a process, called Shaktipat, which involves touching a person on the head or forehead as a way of transmitting *shakti*, or spiritual energy. It is believed that receiving Shaktipat opens up certain energy centres in the brain and body and enables the flowering of self-knowledge or realisation. Muktananda published a fascinating book, *The Play of Consciousness*, describing in detail his Kundalini experiences following Shaktipat received (by a look and the whispering of a *mantra* in the ear) from his Guru. Accounts, such as Muktananda's, make it very clear that some extraordinary infusion of energy and stimulus is involved in authentic Shaktipat, resulting in bizarre internal experiences and altered states. This energy has the ability to spontaneously contort the body into physical postures and movements impossible to perform voluntarily. For example, it can make a person sitting crosslegged on the floor involuntarily and repeatedly kick up several inches off the ground and hop around the room.

What relationship do Shaktipat and the altered states of consciousness, such as bliss and paranormal meditation experiences, have to enlightenment? Presumably Shaktipat can cause some unusual chemical secretions in the brain. The states are certainly seductive and may simulate certain features of the enlightened state (the Sufis call these states Haal and attach little importance to them). The crucial difference is that the enlightened mind is above seduction by experience of *any* kind. It sees all experience as artifact. Only by doing so consistently is it able to *experience reality first-hand*.

What happens to the "I" in this case? It no longer "stands in the way". Its sense of separateness is dissolved. There is nothing to defend or protect, nothing to feel threatened by, nothing to feel separate from.

Notes:

1. For a discussion of some of the philosophical problems related to mind/brain see Churchland, Patricia S., *Neurophilosophy: Toward a Unified Science of the Mind-Brain*.
2. The peculiar feeling of not being the doer of anything has, I suspect, something to do with the complicated relationship between consciousness and time. There is an interesting discussion of this in Roger

Penrose's provocative book, *Shadows Of The Mind*, p.387. Penrose cites experiments which seem to indicate the possibility that consciousness might be just a spectator (or passenger, as Penrose puts it), or a witness to events that have already occurred a fraction of a second before, and this includes one's own apparently volitional acts! The evidence is by no means clear cut and Penrose appropriately highlights the difficulty in arriving at conclusive answers. As he points out, not only do scientists have little knowledge about the phenomenon of consciousness, but fixing the exact time of an event is also somewhat questionable from the perspective of quantum mechanics (at least in the context of consciousness and the observer's entanglement with the event).

Thoughts:
A Sufi Story

Ahmed, the owner of a watch store, was troubled about something. The watches he sold were of the highest quality and they always kept correct time. He noticed one day that one of his better watches was showing the wrong time. He set it right. But when he checked the next day it was again wrong. Ordinarily, he would have assumed that the watch had a defect. However, the watch had been given to him by his teacher, a Sufi master, who had told him that the watch was very reliable.

What did this mean? Ahmed wondered. Could that one watch be correct and all the others wrong? After puzzling over the matter for a few days, he went to see his teacher. The teacher smiled, as teachers often do. "Hah!" he said, "so, you have come to ask me if my watch is correct and all the others wrong. What measure of right and wrong are we to use?"

"Well," said Ahmed, who happened to be an educated man, "I would use some independent means. Something objective that is true absolutely, and not merely relatively."

The teacher smiled even more. "And what might that be?" he asked.

"I am not quite sure," answered Ahmed. "I guess I'd have to ask the physicists for help."

"Good enough," said the teacher, "and what would you do if all the physicists but one agreed on a particular answer and one disagreed?"

Chapter v

First-hand Experience of Reality

There is an interesting English children's rhyme.

Row, row, row your boat
Gently down the stream.
Merrily, merrily, merrily, merrily
Life is but a dream.

Many may have sung it as children. But when we heard or came across it as adults, did it make us stop in our tracks? Awaken us from a dream? Jar our sleep? Life is but a dream. What is the writer getting at?

Awakening is a metaphor that is found almost universally in spiritual traditions. "Realisation" itself is a term which indicates a sudden change in perception or understanding and if it is profound it may seem like awakening from a dream. Is our "ordinary" state of consciousness, the state in which we function and go about our lives all day, a dream state? A second-hand experience of reality?

The neuroscientist, V.S. Ramachandaran, and his colleagues have conducted an interesting experiment, reported in his book, *Phantoms In The Brain*. They used a drawing made of clusters of black dots on a white background. The observer is required to *recognise* some common or familiar figures in the jumble of dots. In the particular drawing used one could, after a few moments of visual inspection, see the picture of a dog. Once the figure of the dog is perceived it jumps out at you every time you look. The scientists studied the subjects' brains during this process using sophisticated scanning techniques. They found that "neurons in the temporal lobes become permanently altered after the initial brief exposure - once the dog has been *seen*".

It is reasonable to presume that in enlightenment some kind of drastic re-synapsing of neural connections takes place, permanently altering one's sense of reality. But "sense of reality" is a vague, almost vacuous, phrase. In this instance, something remarkably *positive* happens. The altered sense of reality brings forth a boundless joy, a deep peace, a feeling that is immensely *freeing*. Hence its characterisation as "liberation". A dream is broken up, leading to a *first-hand encounter with reality*.

What is liberated? Who is liberated? The "I" that had incorrectly identified itself as a particular body and individual with its own internal psychic universe of thoughts, feelings, desires, likes and dislikes, prides and prejudices and so on. The "I" that had taken these artifacts to be real and *indulged* them, allowed them to spin a vast web of personal delusions, separateness, Karma, action and reaction, protection, wanting and grasping.

The Buddha's unparalleled contribution is that he refused to allow any firm ground to the "I". All such ground, he said, is false—an artifact of the mind. I must refer here to my own ideas about sensory perception which I discussed early on in Chapter 1. The chain of arguments I have presented inseparably links our normal texture of cognitive self perception to the *design* of the sensory apparatus. As an analogy, note that what appears to our perception as a motion picture is a continuous series of stills run at a speed exceeding the human eye's capacity to time-resolve contiguous frames. The after-image of each still lingers for a fraction of a second on the retina, so that the running stills create the illusion of motion.

The brain and the sensory apparatus, say vision, is an instrument with fairly well defined limits. It unwittingly assembles discontinuous signals to produce the familiar sense of continuity of existence. This apparatus does not have the capacity to register the vast number of micro-changes occurring in the body. Every micro-second we have a different body. A huge number of cells are different, thoughts are different, chemicals are different, moods have changed. Where is the "I" whose identity and continuity we take for granted?

Seeing this now, what do we do? There is no "I", there is no "we", so who is to do anything? Luckily, the problem is an artificial one. If you have been with me so far and we are in basic agreement on these perceptions, there is no mystery. The brain and sensory systems exist, they operate according to their biological design, this design has limiting and defining parameters, it produces a sense of "I" as a continuously existing entity, whereas in reality there is no such entity. The brain and body operate. That's all that is going on. The subjective sense of "I" is an artifact. But the brain is stuck with the artifact. The "I" is a convention, personal and social, the human brain, under normal circumstances, cannot do without.

Let us therefore be clear about this phantom "I". Instead of "I", or "you", we could perhaps say "this particular brain and body at this location in space-time", objectively call it X or T, and get around the problem. It would be infinitely awkward, but it might give us a way out of the psychological quagmire of "I-ness".

On the whole, however, the strategy would not succeed. We cannot redesign our senses. We shall continue to experience time as continuous. We shall continue to have a sense of personal identity and we shall continue to perceive other individuals as possessing a continuous material and psychological identity, even if we have a mental insight into the sensory illusion.

Then, how did the Buddha get "liberated"? What he realised is that this phantom "I" sustains itself through a cycle of desire, grasping, possessing, owning. And the mind then ends up digging itself deeper and deeper into a quagmire of sorrow, suffering, fear, conflict, desire and malice.

The fact is that there is no ownership in nature—in the Tao. Ownership is a human convention, necessary (?) and useful perhaps for conducting society's affairs. But the phantom "I" becomes real (pseudoreal) by claiming ownership of the body, the thoughts and states of the brain. Hence "my" body, "me", "my thoughts" etc.

Liberation is nothing but simply bringing this cycle of imagined ownership to an end. What happens then? The mind becomes one with life's incredible sensuousness. Sans separation, sans fear of scarcity or lack, sans the need to grasp and hold (as if we could grasp and hold life). Life is experienced at first-hand.

Desire is lack of *closure*. Lack of closure produces the illusion of continuity. When the cycle of imagined ownership is brought to an end, each moment becomes closed—an eternity.

Before I close this chapter I feel compelled to climb down from the heights of enlightenment to the blood and guts reality of our world. The world which seems to revolve around personal ownership, right from the sense of *me*, *my* body, *my* thoughts etc. to *my* child, or wife or husband, *my* country, *my* religion. The primate-human brain is a fearful brain—scarcity conscious, instinctively self-protective, survival driven. The age we live in is the first one in human history when it is possible to understand the compulsions of the primate-human brain against the background of its evolutionary history. The Buddha was not privy to Darwin's Theory, nor were the great Rishis and Sufis. WE are. Not only that, we can now study the operations of the mind-brain in terms of computer-related concepts, programming, genetic codes, memory storage, channels of sense perception, neural chemistry, neural pathways, etc. We have a very powerful window on the primate-human brain and by virtue of this we can stand back from it. Due to this ability, we are, potentially, metaprimate creatures.

But the primate programming of our brain and body is very deep and old. It is going to require extraordinary wisdom, will and relentless application to transform our primate-human brain before it collectively begins to wreak *irreversible* damage on earth. In some Sufi traditions this is called "work"—the unceasing application of self observation, knowledge, insight and practice to alter the deep rooted patterns of primate passions, behaviour and automatic responses of one's own mind and body. In New Sufi thought and practice we make no distinction between spirituality and "evolutionary work".

Thoughts:
More Sufi Poetry

Faceless, the flame of reality stands
Still in its place;
Round and round the chandelier turns
And creates many a face

This couplet by a 20th century Sufi poet, Asgar, presents the idea of anthropomorphism using the image of a chandelier which reflects the light from the flame and shows each observer his own face (the translation is not literal). How does the formless assume so many forms? The poet likens the mind to a chandelier. The formless cannot be perceived. Human cognition can only recognise form. The mind creates these forms.

CHAPTER VI

The Human Being—Reconceived

We live in an ocean of energy. Each of us is like a drop in this ocean. Why do we not feel this ocean around us? Why do we feel ourselves to be separate entities?

In the preceding chapters I have tried to ponder this question and its enormous implications. Somehow the first living cell on this planet formed itself some four billion years ago. A bilipid membrane closed in on itself and a physical and chemical entity with an internal environment different from the external came into existence. The seed of separateness was sown. The cell brilliantly engineered its separateness and identity by learning to homeostatically maintain its internal chemical environment. This enabled it to establish its chemical identity. And then it learned to make exact copies of itself to ensure that this identity would be perpetuated forever!

What an amazing example of artifice, or rather, a series of artifices directed toward the creation and perpetuation of identity.

Separateness is the seed of life. The cell is jealous of its identity and invested in its own separateness.

Some two thousand and five hundred years ago, Gautama, sitting under a tree, had a series of remarkable insights. One of them was about constancy and change. He intuited that suffering is inevitable in a constantly changing world. It is our desire for permanence that causes suffering, he hypothesised. And permanence, or constancy, is an illusion in an ever-changing world. By hanging on to an illusion we cause ourselves suffering. There is nothing but change, said Gautama. We create the illusion of self—an apparently constant entity in the midst of change. In a state of deep meditation, his consciousness penetrated to the very core of matter, and what he found there was change. By the direct observation, or experience, of change at the core of physical reality, Gautama let go of the illusion of self and was enlightened. He was now the Buddha.

In the Buddha's cosmology there is no statis. There are no boundaries. No separation of this from that. To create illusory boundaries in space and constancy in time is to sow the seed of suffering, said the Buddha. It is our desire to perpetuate the illusion of a self—bounded in space and constant in time—that is the cause of our suffering. Desire causes distortion of consciousness, or illusion, and illusion causes suffering. Give up your investment in the illusion of self, and break free from suffering, he taught.

We live in an ocean of energy. Within this ocean we create imaginary islands—our self, other selves, objects. We are so fascinated by this illusion that we do not see the ocean—that it is all one.

> HE is the essence of void and space
> Space exists, but only as a notion
> What is God to show or to say
> If the fish were to ask, where is the ocean?
>
> (quatrain by Iqbal, translated from Urdu)

The apparatus of sense perception in organisms, including us, is so designed as to perpetuate the illusion of boundaries in space and constancy in time. This apparatus perceives selectively. It filters out inputs which would "upset the cart", which would make boundaries ambiguous and the sense of constancy of objects impossible. If the apparatus could register events at an extremely high rate, a few billion bits per second, it would perceive only change, and no constancy. And it would perceive no boundaries, no objects.

If an electron were fitted with a perceptual apparatus to register events occurring in its vicinity at the speed at which events occur at the scale of the electron, it would perceive virtually no constancy. Its own identity would seem unsustainable. If it met a positron, both particles would be annihilated, giving off a ray of energy.

A hoax is programmed into the operations of our brain—a hoax that gives rise to the illusion of separateness. The illusion of identity is an artifice, ingeniously orchestrated by the genes within the cell, to perpetuate the hoax.

Mystics claim that consciousness, like energy itself, is a universal phenomenon. When consciousness gets trapped within an individual brain, it becomes personal. It then perceives through the sense-perceptual apparatus of an individual mind/body and becomes deluded. It identifies with an individual mind/body. What happens in enlightenment is that consciousness is liberated from this identification. There is no longer a feeling of *my* body. This produces a kind of euphoric freedom.

In Chapter 2, I presented the hypothesis that there exists within the human psyche an evolutionary impulse or an evolutionary drive. It is this impulse which finds its fulfillment in the enlightenment experience. The implication of the hypothesis is that there is a sort of instability inherent in the dynamics of human experience. In the normal mode, i.e. in the pre-enlightenment mode, there is a conflict of interest between two fundamental elements of the psyche. These elements can be identified as the Self-Concern System and the Self-Unconcern System. When the force of the Self-Unconcern System becomes too great, the spell of the Self-Concern System is broken. The result is enlightenment.

This proposition says something rather remarkable about the structure of the psyche in the pre- as well as post-enlightenment mode. So that it is not merely a hypothetical explanation of a curious and freak phenomenon. Its purport is that in its normal mode of operation, human consciousness contains an undercurrent of Self-**Unconcern**. This undercurrent is usually subdued. Nevertheless it is there, and it is always making its subdued demands and causing spiritual or existential distress.

Science presents to us a conception of the human being as an organism. According to this conception, since the human being is nothing more than a sophisticated higher primate, the human organism must be subject to the same fundamental drive as other organisms—the drive of Self-Concern. This model has no place for a fundamental drive in opposition to the Self-Concern drive. It cannot account for spiritual distress and spiritual seeking which finds its fulfillment in enlightenment.

According to my hypothesis, the tension between the two opposing drives is the vehicle of evolution in human beings. Some subliminal part of the psyche is wise to the hoax of separation. This results in the condition of spiritual "seeking". The person is responding to a call from beyond, without knowing or being able to cognise what the search is for.

I believe that this "spiritual" element of the psyche is tuned in to the vast energy landscape of the universe. It knows intuitively that every organism and object is embedded in an energy continuum, which is seamless and formless. It is the glorious emptiness which Gautama, the Buddha spoke of and it is the experience of this emptiness which Buddhist meditators seek.

To indicate how the Self-Concern System (SCS) and the Self-Unconcern System (SUS) manifest in conscious human experience, a few characteristics of each are listed below.

Cosmic / Suprapersonal Consciousness	Primate / Personal Consciousness
Self-Unconcern System (Partial list of characteristics)	**Self-Concern System** (Partial list of characteristics)
Unidentified with body or personality	Mind identified with body and personality
No personal needs	"Duality": sense of self as a distinct, disconnected entity.
No point of view	Instinctive self-protection: protection of body and personality.
No causality (no time)	Thoughts, feelings and personal values arise from self-concerned "co-ordinating ego".
Unrelated to circumstances	Personalisation of thoughts, feelings & experience.
Unbounded self	Intense awareness of personal needs and desires.
No concept of fear	Self-interest based strategising. Impoverished ego (sense of dependence on "externals")

Peace and inner stillness as a natural state	Socially defined self-identification (culture, religion, nationhood, etc.)
Perception open to episensory dimensions	Strong emotional attachment to social self-identifiers. Self-expression.
Compassion, universal love	Perceptual field limited to the sensory world. Causality as a perceptual /conceptual mode of organising sensory experience.
Emptiness and Formlessness	Higher human potentialities (creative ego, quest for knowledge, quest for truth, heartful service, evolutionary impulses, etc.).

In the normal mode, consciousness receives inputs from each system and these inputs have to be balanced in order for the ego to function. It is convenient to label this functioning ego, the Co-ordinating Ego. As I conceive it for the purpose of this particular schema of the human psyche, the Co-ordinating Ego is not an entity but a neural pattern or structure formed through an integration of inputs from the two systems. The structure is temporarily stable, but it has an inherent instability, so that growth and evolution are possible. Growth and evolution in this context mean a shift of the point of balance between inputs to the Co-ordinating Ego from the two conflicting systems. Psychological or spiritual growth is a measure of the shifting of the point of balance toward the Self-Unconcern System. The texture of conscious experience changes with spiritual growth. The evolutionary impulse chips away at the Self-Unconcern System. Consciousness moves toward freedom from personalness, seeking to find a home in suprapersonalness. The mystic is one whose Co-ordinating Ego has decisively shifted into the realm of suprapersonalness. There is therefore a sense of completion, of rest and lightness. The suprapersonal is a cosmic dimension. In this mode of consciousness there is a sense of intimate connection with everything.

In the suprapersonal mode there is no causality and no time. In this mode consciousness has the ability to warp space and time. The rules of structuring experience (which is what space and time are) in the Self-Concern mode do not apply to the suprapersonal mode.

At the bottom of the list of characteristics of the Self-Concern System examples of higher-end potentialities are given. When our consciousness is operating at this higher level of potentiality we experience a special thrill, distinctly different from the constricted, intensely self-concerned lower end levels. It is the thrill of self-actualisation. Here the ego is nourished by the process or the activity itself, rather than an expectation of reward or result. When the ego is operating at this outer boundary of the Self-Concern System, it is almost as if it has entered the realm of Self-Unconcern. The "I" has not been disassembled, but there is effectively no thought of self. Energy flows freely and smoothly without damming up in the ego and feeding its characteristic possessiveness. The personal ego—its fear, greed, pride and pettiness, are temporarily decommissioned.

This reconception of the human being suggests marvellous possibilities for conscious evolution.

_____

Part–II

"Who can tell where one person ends and another begins."

Geoffrey Chew,
physicist
— quoted in Capra, Frijof, *Uncommon Wisdom*
(Simon & Schuster, 1988)

CHAPTER VII

Consciousness and Free Will

In Chapter 4, I made a remark in the context of neurophilosophy that this new area of thought provides a framework for discussing some very old and classical problems of philosophy with renewed vigour and precision. The precision comes from asking questions that might eventually lead to scientific discoveries. Thus, both science and philosophy will be enriched.

There is probably no philosophical problem as intriguing as the problem of free will. The problem is very old, but its context and formulation have evolved with the evolution of the knowledge base of human society in the last six or seven thousand years and more particularly in the last three hundred years. Eastern religious worldviews, for example, in the expositions of the *Vedas*, the *Upanishads*, *Bhagavad Gita* and *Vedanta*, address the problem with great philosophical finesse. Its echoes are found in Judaism and Islam and, to a lesser extent, in Christianity. Within the context of religious philosophies the problem is framed in terms of the apparent contradiction between human free will and the omnipotence of God. A number of clever ruses have been invented to resolve the problem. The problem itself arises from the hypothetical omnipotence of a hypothetical entity. Neither hypothesis is empirically verifiable and the debate persists in a strictly abstract form—a classic example of useless philosophical chatter[1].

There is however one important philosopher who, more than three hundred years ago, showed remarkably prescient insight by defining the problem, not with reference to an imaginary entity with imaginary qualities but in terms of the organic form and structure of human life. Spinoza correctly intuited the fundamental problem of consciousness when he wrote: necessities of survival determine instincts, instincts determine thoughts and desires; we think we are free because we are conscious of our thoughts and desires but unconscious of the processes which cause them.

The problem of free will has come back repeatedly to

haunt modern philosophy from at least two directions—one, from the direction of physics and the other, from the direction of psychology and biology, as anticipated by Spinoza. Actually, Spinoza's formulation is strongly influenced by Cartesian philosophy and its determinism. By the middle of the 17th century Descartes had already set the stage for a strictly mechanical conception of the universe. By implication, this conception was extended to include biological processes. What Spinoza's formulation implies is that mental processes have a biological basis and that thoughts and desires which, to our conscious awareness, appear to be within our locus of control are the result of unconscious underlying processes, not unlike the processes of physics.

This is essentially the form in which the problem presents itself today. Is psychology ultimately explainable in terms of biology and biology in terms of physics? Some writers have invoked quantum mechanics to argue against this kind of determinism. If strict determinism is suspect in physics how could it then be applied to biology? The question thus becomes complex and virtually unanswerable within the framework of current knowledge in science. However, some very able scientists are trying hard to bring it decisively within the present scientific framework by making it a legitimate problem in neurobiology. This is exemplified by Francis Crick's "astonishing hypothesis", briefly mentioned in Chapter 4. The thrust of this work is to find the exact biological mechanism of conscious experience. It also seeks to identify, secondarily, areas of the brain where "the feeling of free will arises". Crick cites certain medical cases which apparently involve a "loss of free will" and it turns out that damage to a specific part of the brain is a common factor in these cases. One of these is the "alien hand" syndrome. Crick writes, "for example, the patient's left hand may spontaneously grasp some object placed near it. In some cases the patient is unable to get the hand to let go and has to use the right to detach the left from the object. One patient found that he could not make his 'alien hand' let go by his own willpower, but could make it release its grasp by saying 'let go' in a loud voice."

It may be helpful to use the concept of locus of control to clarify some of the questions involved in the scientific and philosophical debate concerning consciousness and free will. One can easily see that thoughts and desires are not within one's locus of control. They simply arise "on the surface of consciousness", as it were. The process is much too quick to be amenable to conscious control and manipulation. Where we do appear to have control is in making decisions regarding our actions. We may consider various choices and eventually choose one.

There is, I believe, good reason to associate free will with motor control. In the "alien hand" syndrome this control seems to be lost. However, the problem is probably more subtle than this. It seems to me that, while we have no control over what thought or desire might arise in consciousness, we can choose what to think *about*, so that it is not just motor control that is the basis of free will. Similarly, we seem to have control over attention. We can more or less choose freely where to place our attention.

There can be little question that a living organism is deeply and heavily programmed. Exigencies of survival make this essential. In almost all situations every organism, except the human organism in its present context of social evolution, is constrained to act not only extremely quickly but also appropriately, so as not to jeopardise survival and/or other vital interests. This is only achievable through programming, which probably involves a precoded and stored choice of neural pathway and other related processes in the body and brain to produce a specific appropriate action. Without this no organism can survive. We are a partial exception to the rule since much of the time, in our present collective situation, our individual survival is not at stake and the behaviour or action to be carried out needs to be socially, rather than biologically, appropriate. Speed of response is therefore not such a critical factor and the brain may engage in deciding upon or choosing an appropriate response. This, presumably, is what underlies the subjective phenomenon of free will.

Is free will an illusion? The question is immensely meaningful, since a scientific answer might be possible. Even in the context of the present scientific knowledge about the brain, the question is meaningful and of tremendous import. It is difficult, though not impossible, for science in its present form to apprehend the possibility of a non-deterministic macroscopic system. There is an extremely strong and natural tendency in science to assume that every physical event or process is related to a preceding event or process in some form. Even a so-called chaotic system is no exception to the rule. It is this faith which gives science its driving energy. In the context of a scientific analysis of the operations of the brain it is to be assumed that whatever decision or choice the brain might happen to make is the result of some *pre-programmed* algorithms. It is difficult to conceive of "free will" on the part of the brain, which after all is a macroscopic physical system and must therefore behave as such. So goes the logic. I must point out though that there is a minority opinion among scientists which questions the assertion that the brain is nothing more, nor less, than a digital computer[2].

What a momentous thing it would be if science were to show that free will is an illusion. It is almost impossible to apprehend the psychological fallout of this hypothetical discovery. Fortunately, this has not happened and there is no reason for us to anticipate it and consider its implications.

According to the New Sufi thesis, human free will is both a subjective and objective reality. This is really an assumption, but it is not an entirely arbitrary assumption. Rather, the assumption is suggested by the fact that an important characteristic of programmed behaviour is speed of response. The brain is no doubt a computer of some sort, made up of billions of microswitches. There is little question about its hardware. In executing its programmes, that is, its programmed algorithms, the brain works as quickly as any manmade computer. All programmed activity of the brain, including thinking and feeling, is, in terms of our conscious awareness, virtually instantaneous. When, however, we are engaged in deciding something, that is, considering various alternatives, followed by a choice, the process is carried out over a discernible time interval. I believe there is good reason to suppose that decision making is a causally free act. *If it were simply the execution of a programme, it is difficult to see why it should be so slow.*

It is noteworthy that in making choices the brain is under pressure to produce an appropriate response. Decisions that are biologically critical are made extremely quickly and they usually involve motor action. This certainly indicates programmed activity. In other cases, in the human situation, a behavioural response, including a verbal response, might involve some form of introspective consideration. The brain is required to decide on an appropriate response specific to a social situation. The appropriateness of the response might be based on a complex of relationships—some of which may be very subtle. If a learned response is appropriate, it would be produced quickly by executing a stored programme. If, on the other hand, the brain were to find that no learned response is appropriate, or in the interest of the individual, it would be required to generate a response that is inspired by the unique *gestalt* of the situation.

If the brain finds it difficult to quickly produce an appropriate response it would experience some form of existential angst.

From the personal accounts of "enlightened" individuals one gets the sense that these individuals experience no existential angst. In the words of Andrew Cohen, "one always finds oneself at a place from which the perfect response to a given situation is generated"("What Is Enlightenment?" Fall/ Winter 1998 issue). Cohen is speaking here of subjective experience. But it is extraordinary to never experience internal conflict. Here we have a rare combination of the two situations described above. The response is brought forth instantaneously, i.e. without deliberation or conscious consideration, but the response is subjectively judged to be always appropriate. One finds here a new angle on enlightenment. Enlightenment is also frequently described as liberation. In light of the above it appears that the liberation is from existential angst. Choices are made instantaneously and whatever response is brought forth seems perfect. The brain is thus freed from an enormous existential pressure.

Let us step back now and try to integrate the various angles of this discussion. I have made a case to the effect that the speed of virtually all mental events, as well as many behavioural responses, indicates that these are produced by the execution of stored programmes. One has only to introspectively "observe" one's thoughts to realise that thinking is done automatically and could only be the reflection of stored programmes. Similarly, feelings arise quickly and spontaneously. And in most cases behaviour is also programmed. It follows automatically from thoughts and feelings.

The human brain is a primate brain. It has been programmed by millions of years of biological evolution to facilitate the survival of the organism. All organisms on earth must live by their wits. The brain is programmed with strategies for survival in environments that are full of dangers. It is programmed to facilitate survival with cunning and skill under conditions of scarcity. We have inherited this brain from our primate ancestors. More than the brain, we have inherited a mind, distributed throughout the body, which is essentially a primate mind. And we find ourselves now in the extremely peculiar situation of being stuck with a brain/mind whose programmes are generally inappropriate and unsuited to the human situation.

In the last few thousand years, human beings have so mastered their environment through technology that most people on earth can take their own survival for granted. The brain that was programmed for survival of the fittest in a dangerous and scarcity-oriented situation is no longer an appropriate brain. But that is the brain we have.

The ultimate and supreme challenge of human existence is to consciously and deliberately transform our own mind from a scarcity-conscious primate mind, programmed for instant defence, to a human mind operating at a higher "octave of consciousness", virtually outside the normal scheme of nature. This is the challenge which our evolutionary work addresses.

Notes:

1. In the interview with Ramesh Balsekar, quoted in Chapter 4, it is interesting to note Balsekar's unwavering faith in the proposition that everything, including all human actions, are manifestations of God's will. Balsekar is a modern, sophisticated man. Why should he find this proposition self-evident? The only answer I can think of is that he feels he is acting without free will. But even if it is assumed that we act without free will, does it necessarily follow that our actions are manifestations of someone else's (God's) will?

2. Physicist Roger Penrose, whose two books, *The Emperor's New Mind* (Vintage 1990) and *Shadows of the Mind* (Vintage 1995), I have mentioned earlier, has presented sophisticated arguments to the effect that the brain is not a digital computer. He expects that a physical explanation of consciousness and other mental phenomena is to be found in a yet to be discovered physics applicable at the interface between classical and quantum physics. Penrose stays clear of the problem of free will.

Thoughts:
Three Sufi Couplets

These three remarkable Sufi couplets by Ghalib are all taken from the same *ghazal*. One should keep in mind that the couplets of any *ghazal* are not connected and may address unrelated themes. The remaining couplets in this *ghazal* of Ghalib are romantic in nature. But these three indicate that the poet, when composing them, must have been moved by some unusual afflatus which enabled him to probe the heart of classical Sufi thought and condense it into a few words.

> *If the seer, the seen and "the Sight" are all one*
> *In what account, do I wonder, is seeing to be held?*

The terms used in the first line are: *shahud, shahid and mashhud* and the one in the second line, *mushahida*. All derive from the same root, *shahad* (just as *vide* is the root of many words related to vision). By using these similar sounding words the poet not only creates great music but also uses them to delve into the roots of duality. The term *shahud* is inherently untranslatable. It is an enigmatic Sufi term for the "unity of vision" which seems to overpower the *saliks* (Sufi seekers) in the state where they see only God everywhere. I have translated it as "the Sight" to refer to its Sufi meaning. The first line of the couplet is perhaps better translated as: If the essence (or the reality) of the seer, the seen and "the Sight" is the same .... .

> The second couplet I have translated as:
> *To the degree that I believe in the reality of "the other"*
> *Am I removed from my own reality*

This is again a verse about duality. "The other" has no reality. There is no reality but Reality, which is One. And that Reality is who I am.

The third couplet takes Sufi poetry to its highest point.

> *Beyond beyond is that which we take to be Shahud*
> *We are like the man who has awakened in a dream but is still in a dream* ˌ

In the state of *shahud* all that is perceived appears to be God. But this is an illusion, since Reality is "beyond beyond" (another Sufi term). A man who, in a dream, sees himself sleeping and then waking up (*in the dream*) is still in a dream!

One should note that all couplets of a particular *ghazal* are set in the same metre and the second line of each ends in a rhyming word and a repeated end-phrase. This is virtually impossible to reproduce in English translation. Thus a great deal of the beauty of the *ghazal* is lost in translation.

Chapter VIII

Enlightenment vs Evolution:
The Two Paths

There are two distinct traditions within Sufism and it is important to know how they differ and how each one works.

The goal of one of the two paths is enlightenment. The other path is process-, rather than goal-oriented. I will designate the two paths as enlightenment-oriented and evolution-oriented, respectively. The first path is similar to the Buddhist path or the Advaita and Vedanta path. It works on and through the mind and what it aims to accomplish is a non-dual state of consciousness. The underlying assumption of this path is that it is possible to achieve a fundamentally transformed state of mind which is free of the sense of a personal, separate self. The assumption is in the nature of an article of faith. We have the testimony of individuals who have achieved this state. We believe their testimony and assume that if we are lucky we too shall achieve that state. These rare enlightened individuals often become teachers or guides. They become the focal point of a community or group of seekers driven by a mysterious yearning—the yearning to let go of the *burden of self*.

Self-realised individuals often speak of a permanent state of bliss. It seems that what happens is the primate brain undergoes a major transformation. Its characteristic defence reactions vanish. A sudden realisation dawns that the psychobiological self that was being so jealously protected is only an artifact—a creation of the mind. One acquires a foothold outside the sphere of the personal self. The programmed patterns of the separate, personal self lose their power and either quickly or slowly dissipate as the mind reorganises itself and realigns its commitments. One switches, as it were, to a larger self which is recognised as suprapersonal. The repeated insistence of enlightened individuals on the cosmic unity of self, that there is in reality only One Self (Advaita means "not two"), is a natural outcome of this switch. If the personal self is seen as an artifact it ceases to be of committed interest, ceases to have reality and life.

The euphoria of letting go of the burden of self is the euphoria of giving up an illusion—the illusion that the personal self is anything more than an artifact.

The consequences of self-*realisation* are fantastic and radical. The mind becomes quiet. Its subjective universe of thoughts, feelings and desires begins to evaporate. Thoughts, feelings and desires may continue to arise but that is more the result of an in-built momentum, like a spring uncoiling. Gradually, the momentum is dissipated. Then there is a permanent lingering quiet, within which internal and external artifacts of the mind come and go, without leaving much of a trace. Even the personal self-gains no foothold. Its self-indulgence, habits, demands and desires find no ally and eventually die out.

Not many people feel the yearning consciously and strongly enough to devote themselves to the path of enlightenment. The ones who do find the self-centred world of the personal self claustrophobic and seek release into the vast space of the absolute where all is one. Often, they are attracted to a particular teacher by some mysterious pull. A genuine teacher for the path of enlightenment is one whose consciousness has found a home in the vast space of the absolute. In the Sufi tradition realisation of Self is called *Fanaa-fillaah*—the merging of the personal self with the One Self (Allah).

The path of enlightenment in the Sufi tradition can be traversed on one's own. There are several outstanding examples of self-guided realised masters—Rabe'ah Basri, Zu'al Noon, Mansoor Hallaj and Sarmad. But these are exceptions. Very often, seekers are helped and guided by a teacher. Inasmuch as the teacher has realised the Self, the power and light of this realisation touches others in a subtle way, operating beyond the sensory realm, i.e. on episensory and suprasensory levels. Implicit in this Sufi tradition is the notion that the teacher can steadfastly guide the seeker toward the final goal. There is, however, absolutely no guarantee that the goal will be realised.

For some, the lure of enlightenment is overpowering. In

earlier chapters I have referred to this as a natural evolutionary impulse. The assumption was that human consciousness evolves according to a hidden dynamic and the direction of this evolution is from the personal to the suprapersonal. I suspect that the psyche is driven to seek relief from existential angst, or the subtle anxiety associated with freedom of choice. Self-realisation is a psychological condition in which the "burden of self" is relinquished and the dynamic comes to an end. Spiritual "seeking" is a condition of instability in which existential angst is directed positively toward a point of possible resolution. If the angst is negatively directed it results in mental illness.

I must speak now about the other Sufi path. Interestingly, this path does not consider enlightenment as the goal of personal evolution. What it involves is the process of *working on oneself* to create a *transformed* body and mind. This path is evolution-oriented, since a transformed body and mind is an evolved body and mind. Transformation is a relentless, *on-going* process of evolutionary work on oneself[1].

Oneself in this context means the human organism. Like all organisms, the human organism is a programmed system. We saw in the preceding chapter that living organisms often need to react very quickly to situations, many of which involve competing with other organisms for food or protecting oneself from predators. Programming of the brain is designed to achieve this. The brain is a fantastic network of neurons, which form connections with each other to produce coherent electrical activity. Neurons fire tiny electrical pulses and either excite or inhibit other neurons to which they are connected. The coherent activity thus generated represents the intelligent response of the brain to a given stimulus or situation. This activity, which also involves release of specific molecules, called neurotransmitters, at the junction or synaptic cleft of mutually connected neurons, generates the visible response of the body in the form of an action or a verbal response. The brain is equipped to learn, or form new neural pathways, displaying a kind of plasticity, and by this process the organism can change and grow.

The old Sufi teachers did not have this modern scientific knowledge available to them. However, they had remarkably rich intuitive insight into the operation of the human organism. They were great artists, or rather masters of a very high and remarkable art. What they were after is the "awakening" of the organism from the level of nature to a level where the organism is in line with a transcendental order.

They considered nature to be "asleep", and I believe they had a sense that "man" is a part of the natural complex of life and is therefore "asleep". (We find the following passage in Rumi's *Mathnawi*: Originally you were clay. From being mineral you became vegetable. From vegetable you became animal and from animal man. During these periods man did not know where he was going but he was taken on a long journey nonetheless and he has to go through many worlds yet. *Mathnawi III*, Story XVII, quoted in Scott,E., *The People Of The Secret*.)(1). Man's "sleep" is similar to the "sleep" of a butterfly or an ant. All organisms behave according to the principles which make up life—survival, procreation, avoidance of pain, seeking of pleasure. Inasmuch as the organism functions under the automatic operation of these underlying forces it is "asleep".

Where humans differ from this universal scheme of nature is in their capacity to transform the human organism and bring it in line with a higher order. Very few individuals are able to actualise this potential and, therefore, very few individuals are actually "awake". An "awakened" organism is not ruled by the pleasure/pain principle. It does not automatically or reflexively seek its own gain. It is not scarcity-conscious. It is not primed for self-defense and self-protection. In short, it is not an organism in the normal sense of the term.

An "awakened" organism operates out of a different state of consciousness. It is not scarcity-conscious because what it feeds on is not matter, but energy. Western science does not understand the secret of energy. Its understanding is crude. It thinks of energy in terms of calories to be obtained from digestion/combustion of food according to simple thermodynamic principles. It has no way to factor in the mind in its set of equations. It does not understand how energy is gained

---

1 Scott, E., ibid.

or lost without reference to operations of the body.

The Sufi knows that we are a machine that operates on energy. And energy is a mysterious phenomenon. A person's "energy level" has very little to do with the amount of food he or she ingests. This is easily tested. (I have known Sufi masters who ate very little and appeared to have enormous amounts of energy.)

Energy is eternal delight, Blake wrote, and derided "Newton's sleep".

An awakened organism is a transformed organism—one that has evolved to a "higher octave" and is reinforced by energy coming from dimensions unknown to science. A number of things distinguish the transformed state from the realised state. A transformed state is achieved by relentless work on one self, so that the organism's automatic programming is changed in many crucial ways. For example, its natural tendency for self-indulgence is fundamentally transformed. Once this tendency has been conquered it ceases to be a point of struggle. In the absence of this tendency one's thoughts, desires and actions are motivated by a higher sensibility—a natural alignment with a transcendental order. (To give an example, the tendency to overeat can be slowly transformed into an enlightened relationship to food whereby one automatically recognises what the optimum quantity to eat is at a particular meal and spontaneously respects it. The physiological and spiritual rewards made available by this are incorporated into oneself and one lives by this inner sense of balance, health and harmony.)

This particular Sufi path is a truly evolutionary path. It involves intentional, committed and patient reprogramming of primate emotional, thought and behaviour patterns to achieve a metaprimate level of organic functioning. One must note that realisation is different from transformation. A person may become realised without being transformed. In such a case, genuine metaprimate evolution has not been achieved.

_____

Notes:

1. A relatively modern system of working on oneself, where oneself in this context means the self-organism, is exemplified by the Gurdjieff school. See, for example, Gold, E.J., *The Human Biological Machine As A Transformational Apparatus* (2). It is not clear to what extent Gurdjieff was influenced by the Sufis, although it is well known that he had intimate contact with a number of Sufi circles.

---

2 Gold. E.J., ibid..

Thoughts:
Commentary on Mir's Couplet

We are the curtain that lies between
Without us who would hide from whom?

One of the most remarkable things about the *ghazal* is the poet's ability to tell a complete story, or present a whole philosophy, in just a few words. This couplet by Mir, a great Urdu classical poet, is an outstanding example.

The first line itself is highly provocative. The symbolism of the curtain evokes mystery, secrecy, hiding and intrigue. To say that *we* are the curtain elevates the mystery to its highest possibility. The first line does not indicate between whom the curtain lies. A riddle is posed in the line, even though no question is asked. We are tantalised and expect a resolution of the tension. But the second line, instead of offering an answer, itself asks a question. And what a sublime question!

The couplet alludes to an elaborate Sufi theory about Creation. The theory proposes that God created the world in order to experience separation and then ultimately reclaim unity. We were created as part of this drama. We are the curtain. Without us how would this game of hide-and-seek be played?

The great beauty of the couplet is its alluring innuendo. Nothing is explicitly stated. Yet a myth is retold, a story told. Even if we do not know the myth, the dazzling power of the thought implied by the question is enough to stop us in our tracks. And this is complemented by the dazzling intensity of art, as reflected in the words of the question.

I believe the couplet may be even better enjoyed without recourse to its background philosophy. Simply as an implied question answered by a question. We are the curtain that lies between whom? We are the *constituent* stuff of duality. But what does duality hide and from whom? An exquisite paradox.

The Energy Paradigm: Transforming the Primate Brain

Only matter can be owned, not energy. Involvement with matter is the centrepiece of the primate mind.

We live in an incredibly vast ocean of energy. As we saw in Chapter 1, our modes of sense perception are severely limited, so our sensory picture of the world is a thin slice through the vast energy universe. Human vision is tuned to the very narrow band of wavelengths between 0.4 to 0.7 microns (1 micron = one millionth of a metre) right in the middle of the solar spectrum, where solar intensity is the highest. So our visual sense of the world is highly selective and misleading. As I argued in Chapter 1, if our senses were sensitive to energies of all frequencies and intensities the world would look very very different to us. It is even possible that we would not be able to "see" anything at all, since objects would have no boundaries and everything would be more or less fused into one continuous energy landscape. Even more dramatically, it is doubtful that we would have much of a sense of ourselves as a distinct body and a distinct self. Would we exist at all?

Do we owe our existence to the selectivity and limitations of our channels of sense perception? The world which we perceive is literally the creation of our senses and so is our sense of ourselves.

The Yogis called it *Samsara*, the illusion of separate existence.

Matter, in a certain sense, is the key to this illusion. A piece of matter is a bounded island of energy, made visible and distinct by the selectivity and limitations of the senses. We perceive the world as a collection of distinct material objects due to the way our senses work. Once this illusory world is created, our consciousness gets trapped in it and matter becomes our focus of interest.

Most of our social, political and economic institutions are built around control and manipulation of matter. Wars are fought over control of territory. Possession of objects is our criterion of wealth. The entire drama of human consciousness takes place within the material world of *Samsara*.

What we do not realise is that all this is just primate psychology at work. Primate mind is acutely scarcity-conscious. It has evolved over millions and millions of years to help the organism survive under conditions of brutal competition and threats to survival.

We have inherited this mind from our primate ancestors. When we are born our brain is already programmed along the lines of the primate mind. The fact that as a species we have acquired dramatic mastery over our environment is a very recent development in the time scale of biological evolution. The human brain is deeply rooted in primate psychology—in assumptions of scarcity, need for self-protection and control of territory and objects. It is very easy to watch this psychology at work within ourselves. One only has to see how it is reflected in our patterns of thought, emotions and behaviour. These primate-like patterns arise instantly and automatically in the mind.

It is this series of insights that are the basis of New Sufi work. The great challenge of human consciousness and human existence is to transcend the primate mind. All the old and venerable religious and spiritual traditions of the East and the West have been directed *implicitly* towards this challenge. New Sufi thought seeks to provide an explicit framework for this evolutionary work in modern scientific terms.

Once this framework—its assumptions and observations, are clearly articulated, a lot of things begin to fall into place. The inherent nebulousness of religious and spiritual philosophies disappears. The prophets and spiritual teachers of the past were wise people, with a keen intuitive grasp of the nature of primate-human mind, even if they had no notion of the brain's programming or the evolutionary roots of the human species. They were artists of the soul and knew precisely, though intuitively, what they were doing. Unfortunately, to support the practice of evolution beyond the primate mind, they brought in many arbitrary beliefs and ideologies which then devolved into lifeless religious beliefs. Thus the entire tacit basis of evolutionary practice was undermined and the objectives of the practice itself were lost sight of in the maze of childish beliefs centred around notions, such as heaven and hell, afterlife, etc. (We should note in this connection that Buddhism is an outstanding exception. The Buddha placed absolute and total focus on individual practice, with a minimum of myths and beliefs. His eightfold path was directed at transformation of the mind. However, the ultimate goal of Buddhist practice is release from *Samsara*—the illusion of separate existence. This requires a different form of transformation of consciousness.)

In its focus on matter, the primate-human brain becomes stuck in scarcity consciousness. Because the material world around us is finite and relatively small, human beings must compete fiercely to acquire ownership of objects and land. This is classic primate psychology operating in the human context.

If focus is shifted from matter to energy one's relationship to life changes dramatically. It is seen that we live in an infinite universe in which energy flows freely, integrating everything and making the notion of boundaries and the notion of personal possession and control meaningless. When we begin to appreciate that we run on energy and are part of a vast energy landscape the sense of scarcity, and consequent fear, that is characteristic of the primate-human mind is replaced by a sense of plenty. We begin to notice that we get energy not just from food but also from many many things—activities, relationships and interactions that are enjoyable and meaningful, just as we are liable to lose energy from activities and interactions which do not nourish us. We begin to see ourselves as managers and enjoyers of energy and we come to understand William Blake's ecstatic proclamation, Energy is eternal delight.

What a radical transformation it is when our mind begins to think in terms of energy and learns to observe how energy ebbs and flows, how it is created and dissipated, how it is lost and gained, how its imbalance in the body causes distress and disease, how conflicts cause energy to be blocked, how harmony, within and without, causes it to flow freely. A deep and true understanding of energy in the context of human life liberates the mind from fear, anxiety, envy, greed and deprivation.

The calculus of energy is completely different from the calculus of matter. The calculus of matter is the calculus of money, accumulation, ownership and control. It creates war, conflict, inequality, exploitation and ecological destruction. In the calculus of energy there are no servants and masters, no oppressors and oppressed. There is no lack, no need to possess and protect.

As we begin to understand the calculus of energy we make an enormous discovery. The body is an apparatus available to us to move up to a higher "octave" of consciousness. Energy is the medium which makes this possible. For this we must know the right use of energy. To awaken the sleeping organism and to keep it awake means to keep it on a leash with just the right amount of tension, or on a ration of energy that is neither too much nor too little. The body is a bundle of habits. Since it can function adequately by simply executing its stored programs, it can sleepwalk through life. This is how most people function.

When consciousness confronts the mind the process of awakening begins. Through an awakened body and mind we learn the secret of energy.

Thoughts:
Is the Difference Between Past and Future an Artifact?

Suppose you had an experience of precognition. Either in a vivid dream or a sudden flash you saw a scene, or the image of an event taking place, and this scene or event occurred later exactly as you saw it in all its visual detail. The experience leaves you shaken. How could it be possible? Has the future already happened?

To let you in on a well-kept secret, it so happens that the laws of physics cannot account for the future not having already happened. Neither mechanics (classical or quantum), nor relativity makes a distinction between past and future events. (Classical and quantum *statistical* mechanics certainly does, but, as we shall see, that's another matter.)

The second part of the secret is that the basis in physics for making a distinction between past and future is *statistics*—the science of averaging. Now, statistics is a pure artifact. It is a description of average behaviour, arising out of either the inability to mutually distinguish each object or the inability to track each one (theoretically or empirically). Faced with a very large number of small objects, either identical-looking or too numerous for individual tracking, an instrument, such as the eye and the brain, notices only patterns created by group behaviour.

I have made the point in earlier chapters that anything that an instrument notices is due to its design, or more specifically, its *bias*. In our case, our brain notices whatever it values, or whatever it is programmed to *perceive*. This selectivity **produces** the patterns which give rise to our sense of past and future.

Consider a pack of playing cards. Suppose,

the pack is initially sorted out so that all the suits are separated. The pack is now shuffled. Observation of the pack after a few shuffles would show a less ordered distribution. But a little consideration would indicate that our sense of order is an artifact. Any *specific* distribution of cards, e.g., 3,8,6 has the same probability of occurrence as any other, e.g., A,K,Q. But we *notice* the A,K,Q sequence. It jumps out at us. Whereas 3,8,6 is of no particular interest and does not catch our attention.

This is how it is in general. Order and disorder are instrumental artifacts. I suspect it all has to do with the activity of neurons in the brain. Precognition is extremely rare because of the way this activity is organised. In a genuine precognition experience perhaps some circuits get switched within the brain, allowing perception of "future" events. If it is true that the future has already happened then the artifact of the brain's inability to perceive "future" events must be due to the layout of neural circuits.

I suspect that a remarkable revolution is waiting to happen in science. And that this will come about as biology and physics become one, or at least close in on each other. What would be remarkable is that as this happens the attempt to derive biology from physics would be turned around. Theoretical and empirical advances in neurobiology would show that the brain is an apparatus that produces how the universe appears to behave.

So-called psychic phenomena are indeed extremely rare. However, my experience shows that they do occur. Phenomena which science decrees as impossible. In the table in Chapter 6, I have proposed a correlation between such phenomena and the Self-Unconcern System. Persons considered as saints or great spiritual masters have a highly developed Self-Unconcern component. Many also have paranormal abilities.

Part–III

That has always been the pattern of evolution—change never affects a whole population uniformly; in any population there are always a few "mutant" individuals who are "ahead of their time". It may take tens or hundreds of generations for the new property, if it is selectively useful, to become the norm for the species.

Darryl Reanney
Molecular Biologist,
in *After Death* (Avon Books, 1991)

Modesty

Locking eyes with the silent night, I ramble on

The way a lunatic, exposing himself

To a mirror

Might seek proof of the shame of existence.

Keep your eyes down

Speak not

Having been born

Learn the ways of the living

Fill the void of body and being

With solid, imaginary substance

Wrap yourself up in the cloak of name and relationship

Remember, we must hide

The secret of becoming.

(translated from Urdu)

Note:
The phrase in the last line of the original, translated here as the secret of becoming, is "*sirre kun fekan*". This Arabic phrase is taken from a Sura of the Qura'n where Allah says: When We wish to create something We say *kun* (be) and it becomes (*fe yakun*).

Chapter x

Afterthoughts on Parts I & II

I think there are two reasons why a picture puzzle, when assembled, provides such a satisfying sense of closure. One, there are no unused pieces left over. Two, the assembled picture contains all the elements of a recognisable scene.

In the Introduction I said that my quest for answers to basic questions of existence was somewhat like doing a puzzle. What pieces was I trying to fit together, or find a way of fitting together? Some of the questions I was asking are: how and from where does the sense of I arise? Does this sense of I have a neural correlate? By the same token, why, in rare cases, does it "disappear"? What are the implications of its arising and "disappearing"?

The last question is more central to this book. Even if answers to the other questions are hard to find, the last question retains its central position since the implications of the appearing and disappearing of the sense of I seem to me to be enormous. I have more or less laid out my case over a whole series of chapters in Parts I and II. Here I wish only to offer some afterthoughts.

It is an article of faith in science that biology has its basis in chemistry and physics and that quantum mechanics is a tool which, though cumbersome, is applicable to physical processes across the board, including life phenomena. Inasmuch as this is a matter of faith it can neither be defended nor attacked. It is well-known that essentially no aspect of biochemistry is derivable directly from quantum physics. Although some biochemistry could perhaps be explained through principles of chemistry, most of it is merely descriptive. For example, why do the base molecules in the genes form the bonds they do? Why is the structure a double helix?, etc.

The fact of the matter is that there is virtually no fundamental knowledge in biology remotely analogous to physics. Contemporary laboratory methods and computer-based instrumentation technology are a long way ahead of the life scientist's ability to do rigorous theoretical science and this situation will undoubtedly remain unchanged[1]. It is my guess that eventually biology will have to abandon some of its famous axioms. And this will happen when we begin to understand the nature of consciousness.

The basic fault, I believe, lies in thinking of the organism as a material system occupying a well-defined space. This is a prejudice taken over from physics and reinforced by normal sense perception. Yet, as I have tried to show over several chapters, the sensory pictures or forms of external objects produced by the sense-perceptual apparatus are based on highly selective data. To take the normal visual perception of the physical form of another human being as an accurate representation of their physical being is extremely naïve.

Once we give up our fixation on matter and allow ourselves to expand our sense of things into the episensory realms, the world for us changes dramatically. And so does our relationship to it. Or, perhaps even more dramatically, our sense of our own *self* becomes increasingly "soft" and nebulous. We begin to sense our essential connection with the imperceptible world. We become natural mystics.

It is necessary to emphasise that this change in our notion of self is actually a change in the *sense* of self. It occurs at the edge of sense perception. Reality is redefined. As things become fuzzy on the plane of normal conception, other planes appear in view where notions and perception become extraordinarily sharp and formed not out of consensual experience but personal information.

It is at this point that the mystic or the sage falls into a trap. He automatically assumes that this new, extraordinarily sharp vision is "real", whereas the ordinary consensual one is only an apparent view of reality. Such language is characteristic of all mystic and spiritual teachings. The feeling of having at last contacted "reality" is strongly reinforced by the exhilaration and sense of "liberation" which almost always accompany the experience of "self-realisation". Even if the experience doesn't last it leaves an overwhelming taste.

Numerous people who have undergone a vivid near-death experience have reported the somewhat typical feeling of freedom associated with "leaving the body behind". The experience of perceiving, with absolutely no emotional investment, the body one had taken to be oneself is sufficient to alter forever one's total sense of things. The radically altered perspective transforms the "mind's ecology", catapulting consciousness to a plane beyond normal perception. It is not surprising therefore that a large percentage of individuals who have reported such experiences have also reported spontaneously acquiring various types of paranormal perceptual abilities including, in some cases, occasional precognition. Postulation of the Self-Unconcern System in New Sufi thought (Chapter 6) is significant in this regard.

No one of course knows what takes place within the brain during a near-death experience of the kind referred to above. Much of the thought in this book is speculative. But the New Sufi argument is that there is enormous evidence to suggest that *all* perception and apprehension of physical reality is necessarily relative. Alter the design of the sense-perceptual apparatus and this apprehension is altered. Not just the details of sense perception but the way one's complete sense of the world is put together.

But New Sufi philosophy goes further than this. It suggests that the organism's sense and perception of reality is shaped by its implicit *value system*. The gene values itself—its chemical identity. The organism's brain produced under the control of the appropriate genes reflects a similar value system— the organism values itself. Perception comes in as part of this package. The organism perceives selectively, reflecting its values. It reinforces the organism's sense of identity by eliminating perceptual elements that might militate against it.

In self-realisation, as well as some near-death experiences, the individual's value system is abruptly altered. Self-bias, or emotional investment in the body and its mind, is withdrawn. One ceases to identify emotionally with the body and its mind. Surely, this drastic alteration of emotional behaviour must have a neural correlate.

What New Sufi thought proposes is that the experience of the mystic and the sage, as well as the experience of the normal human being, i.e. the condition of strong personal association with the body and mind, are *both* physical states of the brain. It is meaningless to say that one is more real than the other. It is also meaningless to say that one is a more correct "view" of reality than the other.

Thus the tenor of the debate changes. The question becomes one of choice of values. Do we wish to value emotional identity with the body and its mind or do we wish to be free from it?

Suppose we wish to be free from it. Surely, the wish or the decision doesn't set us free. Presumably, some deep neurological change needs to take place for that to happen.

We do not understand in any important way how our brain works, how it perceives what it does and why it doesn't perceive what it does not. The mystery only deepens when we try to bring science and mystic experience together. I wish to recommend humility to both the scientist and the mystic. No human being would probably ever know where the organism's (or the gene's) bias in favour of its own form comes from. Or, even more mysteriously, what drive is it within the human psyche that so ardently seeks liberation from this bias.

Notes:

1. Biological science in the twentieth century has followed a remarkably different course than the physical sciences. Virtually all the major theoretical work in physics, including relativity and quantum mechanics, was done independently of experiments. Almost always, experimental confirmation followed the framing of hypotheses and construction of the mathematical theory, even though the initial impetus might have had its source in anomalous laboratory data. In biology and medical science laboratory techniques, such as electron microscopy and magnetic imaging, have almost completely guided theoretical research. This is remarkably evident now in neurobiology. All the current models of the brain are directly or indirectly based on various forms of imaging.

Thoughts:
A Critique of Science and Mysticism

Suppose that in the story on page 73 we replace the deviant watch with the *mystic*. He is an individual who disagrees rather fundamentally with the rest of us about what is real. The modern mystic, Baba Gonush, is reported as saying, "In my world time does not pass".

How is one to know what is real? Should we decide by consensus? The scientist would say, "Let the instruments decide". The idea is that since instruments are "unbiased", they constitute an unbiased measure of reality.

To this the mystic would say, "Yes, but an unbiased measure of what reality?" His argument would be that the reality we believe in is real for us because it is consensual and sensory.

The point of the Sufi story on page 73 now becomes apparent. WE are the instruments!

We agree on our perceptions of reality by *standardising* our sense perceptual apparatus. "Errant" data are screened out and it is ensured that the common denominator of every "normal" person's sensory perception would decide what is real.

Our "reality" (reality by consensus) is a poor reality. Its poverty is evident in a number of ways. The most telling of these is that it does not satisfy us. Some part of our psyche sees through it and this faculty of our mind knows that there are vast areas of human experience outside and beyond the bounds of standardised, consensual, sensory reality. And that these other regions of experience are valuable, meaningful and essential for human wholeness.

Any philosopher of science who is also a Sufi or a mystic would assert that the human perceptual apparatus is an instrument. In experimental scientific work we are not merely standardising laboratory instruments but also our personal and individual instrumentation. Because, in the final analysis, WE perceive and interpret the readings of the instruments. If our perceptual and cognitive processes are not standardised the readings of the lab instruments would be useless.

Suppose we think of a mystic, or a psychic, or someone (could be any of us) with a high level of episensory perceptual ability, as an instrument. This instrument appears to register certain signals which other human instruments apparently do not. Should this data be considered erroneous or phantom—generated, like noise, by the system itself? Or, might we conclude that this instrument is more sensitive than the others, better tuned and with a higher capacity?

Perhaps the most important point of the argument is that no *instrument* can know anything about reality, i.e. what is real and what is not. It has no means to do so. Nor can a group of instruments, any number of them, get together and determine this.

Consider the following situation regarding human sense perception. We have faith in our normal sense perception since we constantly test it. The outside world provides the necessary "objective" data to distinguish sensory fact from fantasy. If we see an object in front of us and approach it, we expect to find it there when we reach it—solid and tangible to our touch. If we do not, we would conclude that our original vision was an optical illusion. Thus reality and illusion are clearly distinguishable to us in sense experience.

Assume, however, that a person sees an aura around someone's head. This cannot be touched and its reality confirmed. The fact that 99.99% of the people do not see auras has no bearing on whether or not the aura is really there. Maybe their visual instruments are not as sensitive. By the same token, the fact that auras do not show on a photograph cannot be a deciding basis. All instruments, including a normal photographic camera, are designed to operate within a limited range.

Suppose, however, that an instrument is available which has been designed to operate over all frequencies and intensities of photon (electromagnetic) input. If the aura fails to show on this instrument as well, are we justified in concluding that it does not exist?

There is absolutely no law of physics that says that the laws accepted as true by physics at any time, or the sum of facts known to it at any time, are complete or even correct. If such a law were to be proposed, it could not be tested.

Science cannot say anything about what it does not know, any more than an instrument can say anything about what it does not register.

I believe what has gone wrong in science, in terms of its philosophical fallacies, is that the role of the human perceptual and cognitive apparatus in a science such as physics was not recognised. Physics has been pursued independent of biology. This is perfectly all right. The only thing is that it is not equipped to make statements about reality.

But I should like to make the point that, by the same token, mystics too have no right to decide, whether for themselves or for others, what is real and what is not. Their perceptual and cognitive apparatuses are also instruments. And no instrument can say anything about reality. (There is a school of thought in Sufism associated with the Naqshbandiyah Order, which asserts that the mystic belief in non-duality is founded on the mystic's personal vision and experience and is not a reflection of actual reality, in which Creator and creation are distinct and separated. However, the Naqshbandiyah philosophy of duality is itself a belief—no less arbitrary in its assertions about reality than any other system. Both duality and non-duality are interpretations imposed upon reality based on inner experience.)

With rapid advances in the neurosciences it might be possible to know, at least in a crude manner, how the human perceptual and cognitive apparatus works. Perhaps, then, we will be able to understand such things as how this apparatus assembles its perception of space and time. And then maybe we would be able to understand why in Baba Gonush's world no time passes, whereas in ours it does. Maybe something in our heads strings together successive and discontinuous frames of visual perception to produce the sense of continuous reality. For the Buddha it was different.

CHAPTER XI
Spirit Blues

"The blues"—a dark and dismal cloud cover which descends at its own whim and wraps its dreary arms around us. Its power lies in our inability to understand what it is about, why it strikes, how it works. To look it in the face and read its features is to turn its power upon itself.

Some blues are spirit blues. They dog the hapless traveller on the evolutionary path, who can see so clearly with his spirit eyes the golden sun beyond the hills. But a hard, rocky path chews at his feet, the world demands its daily dose of detail and drudge. The blues come from our inability to fly and not have to walk the rocky path of human life.

There's an angel in us trapped in an ape's mind and body. We are both—the angel and the ape. The ape—the primate part of us—embodies the compulsions of biological life. It is concerned with itself. It fears, defends, attacks, wants, looks out for itself and its kind. It operates on blind Darwinian logic. The angel—the metaprimate part—operates outside the Darwinian sphere, indeed outside the sphere of matter and objects. It is unconcerned with itself. It seeks union, rather than separation. Recognises love and not fear. It is cosmic and has no self-bias.

Who gets the spirit blues and why? Not the angel. It's the mind that does—the mind that wants to evolve and reach beyond the primate self. This urge, often subtle, acts like an upward force. It is buoyant, it lightens.

Depression comes when the evolving mind, in its attempt to become metaprimate, is pulled down by the force of primate self-concern. Or more correctly, when the mind becomes consciously or unconsciously aware of its struggle to rise against that force and is unable to do so.

There are numerous manifestations of this counter-evolutionary force all around us. Most of our social and economic institutions are shaped by it. It is only very recently, on the time scale of evolution, that our species has reached a point where physical safety of the individual organism can be taken for granted. This is unprecedented in the history of earthly life. The mind, faced with this extraordinary situation, is forced to direct its primate reflexes of fear, defense, attack and conquest toward psychological fronts—protection of identity, beliefs, institutions, biases.

Our mind is a deeply confused mind. Its attempt to understand itself has only just begun, made possible by the re-allocation of psychic energy from concerns of physical safety to areas of the brain involved in higher cognition. With the explosive growth of science in the last few decades, the sum of human knowledge has suddenly become extremely unbalanced. We know a great deal about the physical world and are able to manipulate it very effectively. But our knowledge of our own souls remains dangerously limited and may even have dwindled in the last century. Unless a new set of sciences and arts, concerned with the mind and the soul, are able to help us understand and integrate our natural self-bias with our unusual spiritual need to transcend bias we may be in great danger from our own unbalanced knowledge.

Some of us feel the spirit blues more than others. There is a simple way to tell if one's blues are spirit blues. Is one pulled down by manifestations of primate self-concern, defensiveness, aggression, fear and greed within oneself and around one? Does one feel one's spirits lift by manifestations of peace, contentment, lack of personal bias within oneself and around one?

Does one feel one's spirits lift by being around people engaged in personal evolution toward a metaprimate level? A level where the demands of body and soul are not counter-poised but one.

The way to beat the spirit blues is to engage, heart and soul, alone and in mutual support, in this great human challenge.

Thoughts:
Demystifying Meditation

If I were asked to name the three most poorly defined words in English, I would say, God, spirit and meditation. Perhaps in the case of the first two the lack of a clear concept is, in some sense, a virtue, but it is hard to see anything good about the confusion and muddle-headedness surrounding meditation.

In our work we make a distinction between meditation and sitting for meditation. The latter is within our locus of control. The former is not. Meditation, in our approach, is defined as a "neutral" state of mind and body. The analogy of a spring is useful here. Under the action of an external force the spring would either go into tension or into compression. Both are states of stress. When the force is removed, the spring regains its neutral length and its natural stress-free state. Meditation is a natural, stress-free state of mind and body—a state of balance, equilibrium, equipoise and rest.

How is this state attained? The answer is: just like a spring, the mind-body system will seek its neutral state and will achieve it *if it is not prevented from doing so*. This means, if it is left alone.

Take the analogy of sleep. At night, when a person lies down in bed, the human mind-body system tends to fall asleep naturally, unless it is not in need of sleep or something prevents it from falling asleep. The body requires rest and equilibrium and it receives this through sleep, which is a condition in which mind and body are left alone.

So it is with sitting for meditation What

we do is to settle into a position of physical poise and balance—sitting cross-legged, with or without a cushion, with the back upright. This is a posture of equipoise, dignity, stability, balance and peace. With the body perfectly balanced, it is easier for the mind also to settle into a state of rest. All we need to do is do nothing that would interfere with this process of the mind seeking a state of rest and balance.

In practice, this means leaving one's thoughts alone. If we follow the thoughts with interest this tends to generate reactions in the body. Feelings and emotions will arise and the system will consume energy and experience stress. To allow mind and body to experience a state of minimum energy consumption, and therefore a state of complete rest, we leave it, i.e., its thoughts and sensations alone, with full intent and awareness. The cross-legged posture, with the back upright, holding the body in a relaxed state of equipoise, is inherently a position of intent and awareness. The intent and awareness become particularly sharp in this case, since the objective is not to give any importance to the *content* of experience.

This last point must be well understood. Again, the analogy of sleep is useful. *The purpose of sleep is not to have great dreams*, which are the conscious content of experience during sleep, but to rest and wake up feeling rejuvenated. Similarly, the purpose of meditation is to experience a neutral state, while being conscious. The content of any experience one might have in body or mind is irrelevant to the purpose.

Do we require a technique, or a set of techniques, to keep awareness from getting involved with thoughts and chasing them around? If it helps to use a technique, such as the repetition of a word or a point of focus, like the breath or a part of the body, that's fine. Quite often a technique like this can help keep the attention steady on a sensation or a repeated sound and thus allow the mind to rest. By experimenting one may be able to find what works best. The idea is simply to allow mind and body to experience rest.

Hence, what we actually do is sit. Settle into the posture described, close our eyes and let the mind-body system find its neutral state.

The benefits of sitting for meditation regularly every day do not need to be elaborated. As in the case of sleep, benefits to the health of mind and body are enormous. But other benefits may also be experienced. The equanimity and equipoise spill over and keep us centred under all circumstances.

How to leave one's thoughts alone? Thoughts are quickly changing patterns. Awareness has a natural tendency to notice change. Attention is automatically drawn to the running succession of thoughts. What helps the meditation practitioner is the understanding that thoughts are not one's thoughts. They are just thoughts. They don't belong to anyone. If we are clear in our understanding that what we want is to experience rest and rejuvenation, then with a little practice it becomes possible to enter into a state of self-unconcern when we sit for meditation. The spiritual benefits of this are very great.

Perhaps it is all a question of what we value. Attention is automatically directed to whatever is valued. If we wish to value thoughts while sitting for meditation, then we will attend to them and take interest in them. However, if we value peace and rest and wish to experience this in meditation our attention and interest will not follow the thoughts around and get caught up in them.

The experience of self-unconcern, even if it lasts only a few minutes, places us in the right relationship to Creation. We realise then that we don't own anything. Nothing belongs to anyone. Sometimes Sufi teachers like to make a distinction between consciousness and awareness. Consciousness arises from a sense of "me". "My" concerns, "my" thoughts, "my" desires, etc. The self in this case acts through a "me" and this generates consciousness out of the phenomenon of awareness. In meditation we are not concerned with "me". We disown *all* artifacts.

Chapter XII

Deep Questions for Neuropsychology

Oliver Sacks, Clinical Professor of Neurology at the Albert Einstein College of Medicine, has presented, in a series of highly readable books, several fascinating case studies of individuals who have suffered physical damage to different parts of the brain and, as a result, undergone dramatic change in behaviour and consciousness. With the help of such cases and many other techniques neuroscientists are beginning to gradually understand how the normal human brain is organised and how disease and damage can upset this fragile organisation.

The first important discovery is that the brain is indeed a machine. It processes data and regulates physiochemical processes within the body. This regulation is carried out by two means—electrically and chemically. The brain sends electrical signals through a vast network of nerves which activate appropriate responses in various parts and organs of the body. At the same time the brain is a gland. It produces a large family of chemicals to regulate its own electrical processes, plus it releases many chemicals into the blood stream which travel all over the body and bind to various sites within the organs.

Evolutionary biologists have very good reasons to believe that the brain has evolved over billions of years as a delicate, fine-tuned central processing and regulating system to help each organism survive in the midst of ever-present danger and intense competition for food. The anatomy of the human brain clearly reflects this evolution. It has three fairly distinguishable parts— the old brain, mid-brain and the forebrain. At the risk of great simplification, one might say that these segments of the human brain are, respectively, the seats of instincts, emotions and higher cognitive abilities. It is observed that after birth growth in brain size, represented by the ongoing formation of new neural connections, occurs exclusively in the forebrain. The brain learns by establishing neural pathways to quickly and automatically generate responses that have been tested through experience and found desirable. This enables the organism to survive continually in situations where speed of action and response are critical.

Neuropsychology is an emerging, highly complex science. Its function is to bridge the gap between neurobiology and psychology. As can be seen from Oliver Sacks' and V.S. Ramachandran's books (see Bibliography), a great deal of abnormal psychology is correlated with brain pathology. The pathology occurs in the form of various changes in the brain's chemical and electrical functioning. One of the most spectacular scientific developments of the last quarter of the twentieth century is the ongoing discovery of molecules produced at the synaptic clefts of neurons which seem to regulate our moods, our feelings of well-being, our highs and lows and, subsequently, our behaviour. It is becoming clear that the brain is an incredibly intricate chemical system and minor changes in its chemistry can have major consequences. Thus, very small doses of certain drugs can induce unusual experiences, alteration of perception, euphoria and hallucinations.

However, our notions of pathology are necessarily "normative". They are grounded in socially and culturally sanctioned patterns of feeling and behaviour. Every society regulates individual conduct and internal experience in the interest of protecting its institutions and power structure. But beyond this, it appears that nature itself has designed deep seated mechanisms to ensure that its fundamental imperatives are upheld. The instinctive reflex in every organism to protect its own physical and chemical identity is certainly the most fundamental of these imperatives.

Mysteriously, in enlightenment this imperative is subverted. Unlike suicide, however, the subversion takes place in a curious fashion. A powerful feeling arises that one is not this body nor its states of mind.

Should this curious self-distancing be considered pathological? What if it is accompanied, as it frequently is in enlightenment, by unusual lightness, joy, sense of freedom and deep affection for all creation? By the same token, this self-distancing frees the mind from prejudice, pettiness, allegiance to a specific belief system or their sanctity. This is socially "dangerous"—it is against social norms. But it also subverts the design of nature in a fundamental way because life perpetuates itself as a result of its attachment to its own *artifacts*, and enlightenment, or for that matter spiritual growth, acts to break the spell created by this attachment.

A self-realised mind is free of fear since it is not attached to anything that needs to be protected.

I believe that the understanding of the mind's attachment to life's artifacts, for example, physical and chemical identity is a scientifically meaningful question. Spiritual growth appears to be synonymous with a weakening of the hypnotic spell of this attachment and enlightenment is its final shattering. The fact that this weakening is accompanied by a delightful feeling of lightness and freedom should be sufficient to stimulate its neuropsychological study. But I believe such a study is warranted for far more important reasons. It might be essential in understanding how the primate-human brain needs to evolve, biologically and psychologically, to become a metaprimate brain—a brain that our species *must* develop in order to survive and evolve.

———————————

Thoughts:
The End of Indulgence

What are the things that I like and do not like about the New Age? There are many good things, which seem to me to be evolutionary, in the sense implied in this book. There is a willingness to expand horizons beyond established belief systems and an overall recognition of the relevance of the imperceptible, something that Western science has vigorously attempted to banish. In reaction to this perhaps there is overreaction and one is immediately struck by excesses in the New Age that almost appear mediaeval.

But I think it is more important to see what's going on at the level of the heart than of the mind. Is there more genuine affection among people, transcending traditional me-thou dichotomies based on externals—colour, nationality, beliefs, culture? Are people helping each other out more, sharing more, possessing less or being less attached to possessions?

I do not see many signs of less indulgence of self. In fact, there is probably much more. It seems that new forms of entertainment and indulgence have been discovered. So much of what passes for spirituality appears to be tainted with indulgence—the focus is irrevocably on "me".

The form of spirituality which the Sufis and other genuine systems teach has no room for indulgence. The teacher sees to it that you will work to give up self-indulgence, not deepen it. The self is the first and last icon the seeker is challenged to break and one must keep chipping away at it throughout one's life. As pieces fall away, there is a growing sense of freedom and lightness.

CHAPTER XIII

The Making of a Metaprimate Human

Years ago I participated in a series of workshops on a form of dance and movement work which its originator, Emilie Conrad Da'oud, has named Continuum. Continuum creates an unusual somatic context in which the participant frequently has the experience of not being a solid body at all, but rather a fluid or a field that ebbs and grows and pulsates with the energy of consciousness. When this core experience occurs the mind's relationship to not only the body but also to itself and everything around it is drastically altered. Space and time become entirely non-linear and the apparent solidity of the physical world begins to change.

What also happens as a result of doing prolonged Continuum work is an extraordinary softening of thought forms. The mind's fixation on matter is given up. And along with this, one's total experience of life—patterns of perception, sensory experience, relationship to other bodies and objects, is gradually transformed.

Continuum is one valuable tool in the making of a metaprimate human.

A metaprimate being lives in a field of energy. That is to say, her perceptual experience extends into the episensory and the boundaries which appear to exist around solid bodies lose their objective existence. As fields, objects, and especially bodies, interpenetrate.

One of the major consequences of a switch from fixation on matter to an actual sensation of the energy around us and within us is a radical change in both thought structures and the actual moment-to-moment experience of life. In a world made up of energy and not matter, *nothing can be owned*. Not even one's own body. Thus the very idea of "my" body becomes devoid of experiential meaning. Naturally, with this radical shift, nothing can ever be the same.

We are not material systems. Matter is, in reality, only

energy. It has captured a central place in our perception of the world because our senses are designed to pick out, through reflected light or touch, those particular configurations of energy which we call matter. By refining our perception and inner experience we begin to realise that we transact with each other and with the vast physical and biological universe around us through continuous exchanges of energy.

Our perception, thus, moves from a "hard" universe to a "soft" universe. And we see ourselves as embedded in this soft universe. Our perception of matter is seen as a sensory artifact, as is our perception and experience of our body.

Billions of years ago on primordial earth, a group of organisms arose, from a spontaneous or an orchestrated organisation of chemicals. The first cells that arose were the first organisms. This organism had several extraordinary characteristics. One, it had a physical boundary in the form of an encircling membrane, two, it had a chemical identity, i.e. an internal chemical composition that was different from the surrounding chemical environment, three, it had the ability to identify itself in terms of its physical territory and chemical identity, and four, it had the ability to briefly sustain itself and split into two exact copies of itself, thereby perpetuating its own identity forever.

To sustain its chemical identity in the face of processes which tend to make everything uniform, the cell requires energy. It obtains this by metabolising certain chemicals taken from its environment. As a result, these one-celled organisms begin to compete with each other for access to the chemicals which constitute their food. In this way, an ongoing drama of life is set up which continues on earth to this day, made increasingly complex by billions of years of biological activity, but retaining the fundamental imperatives exhibited by the very first living cells.

What this very succinct telescoping of life's essential characteristics means is that every organism operates on the basis of a perception of its own identity and the will to preserve it. What it also means is that every organism places itself first, and in the midst of a limited supply of food, considers every other organism a competitor and threat. Since multicelled organisms tend to feed on each other, actual and direct threat to life is an ever-present reality for all organisms. Fear is a biochemical device invented by life to facilitate the organism's defence apparatus.

What might we learn from this telescoping of life's imperatives? One, that the distinction of self, in relation to non-self, is an artifact of perception. Two, fear of "the other" is a fear of the competitor and possible life-threat. Three, scarcity engenders competition and fear. And four, human beings, by solving the problem of scarcity of food and the problem of threat to human life from other organisms, now stand at a completely new place in the saga of evolution.

It is a very bizarre situation. For human beings now, there is no scarcity of food and no threat to life from the "other". Yet, our fear of the "other" is deep and often assumes frightening forms.

We know the roots of this unreasonable fear. Can we conquer it?

The gradual, but progressive, conquest of fear of the "other" is called spirituality. As spiritual awareness deepens, the perception of self and the "other", and their mutual separation, is gradually altered—not only cognitively but also emotionally. The boundaries of self expand and more and more of the "other" is included in the self. This process appears to come to an end when the distinction between self and the "other" disappears, emotionally and cognitively.

The metaprimate mind begins to evolve as soon as our imagined sense of scarcity is let go. As we have seen, this sense is a carryover from our evolutionary past. It manifests in the present through the human mind's addiction to matter. This addiction can be gradually overcome through the consistent recognition that our best and deepest joys involve those exchanges of energy in which there is deep contact. These exchanges are not subject to the laws of matter, or to the laws of scarcity. By actualising this recognition and giving ourselves to deep contact with all that exists we are liberated.

"Nearly Final" Thoughts

Let me offer now some "nearly final" thoughts.

I mentioned at the outset the Sufi hypothesis that there is in the human psyche an evolutionary urge to develop slowly, but decisively, to a point of ultimate freedom and that freedom is liberation from the dichotomy of "me and thou". This book might be considered a long commentary on this doctrine. I have tried to make the doctrine intelligible from the point of view of modern science and, in doing so, I have tried to show how the power of science and the power of mystical insight can be combined to enable human beings to reach an extraordinary level of personal development.

It occurs to me now that perhaps a single philosophical paradigm might be used to put all this together and that paradigm is implied by the idea of wholeness. The split of the whole into "me" and "thou" produces the spiritual, or psychological, dynamic of the urge to reunite and become whole again.

Let me try to convey very briefly my "sense" of what might be involved. It is, fundamentally, our bodies that divide us into "me" and "thou". The mystic's disowning of his or her body, as in the assertion, "I am not my body", is an appropriate psychological response to the urge to become whole, i.e. disidentify with that which is responsible for (the sense of) the dichotomy. The "seeker" is one who feels a yearning for wholeness or (re-)union. The mystic experience is an experience of wholeness. But wholeness is not made up of experiences, since experience is still personal. The liberation from "me" and "thou" of which the sages speak is a lasting release into wholeness.

I do not find it surprising at all that enlightenment or self-realisation is a complex psychological and, ultimately, neurological phenomenon, often triggered by direct association with an enlightened teacher. The best historical example is probably the Buddha. It is believed that he used a method of transmission of insight through "progressive illumination", sometimes enabling one or more individuals to achieve enlightenment in a single discourse. I believe the illumination was brought about by progressively seeing through the layers of "artifact" which cover the nothingness which, the Buddha taught, is left when *all* artifacts are removed. Gautama was not privy to the discoveries of 20th century physics. But he somehow saw that physical substance is an artifact. Of course, before him, the authors of the *Vedas* had written at length about the unreality of the physical world, noting that matter is an outward, and ultimately unreal, manifestation of energy, or in even more abstract terms, an unfolding and spreading of "vibrations". Thus there already was in the Buddha's time a historical and philosophical tradition of considering the material world, or our sensory experience of matter, as an artifact. Gautama's uniqueness lay in his ability to transmit illumination through discourse and *personal presence*. There was, without a doubt, a transmission of insight and illumination to those who were ready brought about by his personal presence. If this were not so, reading his sermons would be sufficient for illumination.

Is the direct experience of the Void which the Buddha spoke of the same as wholeness? I think we should be careful here. It is true that in the Void there is no me-thou dichotomy. And when there is no "me" there can be no personal fear. This may be considered liberation. But something is missing here which, I believe, the Sufis (or rather some Sufis) were aware of and they tried to intuitively supply the missing piece. Yet, I think the Sufis too didn't quite get it right.

The missing piece is love. While there is no place for fear in the Void, there is also no place for love. The Buddha advised compassion. In fact, compassion is the natural result of illumination. Because, one then intuitively understands the mechanics of *Samsara* and the basis of personal fear and thus cannot help but feel compassion for those trapped in it.

However, love is a different thing altogether. It is interesting that, with the exception of the *Gita*, hardly any Hindu religious text has much to say about love. The ancient Hindu teachers were not interested in human emotions. Truth was more important than love. When the soul realises its own eternal truth it is liberated. I think the Buddha also taught on the same lines. In his teaching the liberating insight is *not* generated through love.

Now, the 9th to 11th century Sufis were given to raptures. Love for them was an emotion that was central to the process of (re)uniting with God. It was the vehicle which took them there. But love of what? These Sufis might say love of God. But God is only a concept. So are we talking about love of a concept? That cannot be. What we are talking about is the great lure of wholeness. Wholeness in which the "me" is forgotten.

I believe these Sufis were seduced by their states of ecstasy and pangs of love. They projected their pangs of love on to an unknown object of devotion along the lines of the normal human experience of love of a person. But this love of "God" is itself in the realm of duality! Love presumes a "me" who feels the love. Without it there is no love. The Sufis should have realised this from the fact that when the so-called "*fana*" (union with God) is achieved the love doesn't cease. Only personal fear and self-concern do.

There is no compelling reason to bring "God" into this. What I have suggested is that the yearning for wholeness is a natural "higher" human (metaprimate) instinct. And love in its many human manifestations is the experience of, briefly or for longer times, stepping around the me-thou dichotomy.

I think that something physical happens in the experience of love. Not only in the brain but also in our experience of the envelope of energy which is our physical self. In love the individual energies interpenetrate. The rigid form and separation implied by matter are overridden in this experience of interpenetration of energies.

The me-thou dichotomy is sustained, if not created, by the organism's sensory experience of matter, which is an artifact of its sense-perceptual system. I think this holds at all levels— from the cell to large organisms. But there is probably a critical size or threshold below which the experience of matter cannot be sustained. For example, if an electron were equipped with a sense-perception system it would *not* experience or perceive a material world.

It seems to me that our brains are wired to operate with the me-thou dichotomy as a basis of experience. And I mean wired in a fairly literal sense. There are probably precise neural routes associated with it. But there may also be some chemical processes involved in the clefts and these may control the configuration and weighting of the synapses, including timing and synchronisation.

What an interesting challenge it would be for neurology to discover the neural structures associated with the me-thou dichotomy. I strongly suspect that in enlightenment some type of crucial resynapsing occurs in these structures. Along with this an umbilical cord between "I" and "me", so to speak, is broken. (Dr.V.S.Ramachandran and colleagues have reported *observing* resynapsing in instances of suddenly perceiving a hidden form in a jumble of dots and patches, see Ramachandran, (1998) p.239. Apparently, neurons in the temporal lobes are involved in such rapid visual learning. There may be similar specific sites involved in enlightenment, or what John Wren-Lewis calls, the eternity experience. Perhaps there is a variety of enlightenment experiences, as Wren-Lewis himself suspects. Ramachandran believes that many mystical experiences involve abnormal activity in the temporal lobes. However, only some experiences may result in "learning", i.e., permanent alteration in neural connections.)

However, fascinating as all this might be, the question is: what does it mean for us and the human species in general? I have tried to show that the me-thou dichotomy which holds so very uncompromisingly for other organisms is not quite applicable in the same form for human beings whose physical survival is no longer threatened by competitors and predators. But our brains are essentially primate brains. They are wired to respond to situations extremely quickly on the basis of stored programmes. And many of these programmes are inappropriate and destructive in our case. Where scarcity is the primary fact of life for all other organisms, for us it is an assumption we unconsciously make and have the choice to consciously reject. (We wish to eventually reach a place where the unconscious assumption of scarcity is replaced by the *unconscious* assumption of sufficiency.)

The form of Sufism I am proposing combines love and knowledge and makes them one. Both help to reprogramme our primate brain. Knowledge helps us understand the roots of the me-thou dichotomy, the roots of fear, conflict, self-interest, control, ownership, ecological destruction, mindless consumption and so on. Love gives us an experience of sufficiency and abundance outside the realm of material finiteness.

In love individual energies interpenetrate. The separation and boundedness (me-ness) implied by embodied existence is relaxed. We move closer towards wholeness. This is a clue to how it can be done. Interpenetration of individual energies is something that can be allowed to happen if we wish to do so. The experience of love is possible by choice. And along with this, the elimination of fear, greed, insufficiency, want. As we welcome this experience more and more and allow it to happen we discover beauty and wholeness. We become free. We are no longer we, as we have known ourselves to be.

———————————————

Let the Wine Cup Be

Let the wine cup be empty.

Beyond wine and song, the heavenly server

Comes bearing the poisonous cup

Which kills the bliss of self-indulgence

Leave the Sufi in his house of ecstasy

You and I, we have work to do

Beyond pleasure and pain, wine and song

A million years did Nature work

To make man

But we, you and I, have but a lifetime

To become more than man

(translated from Urdu)

The Power of a Metaphor

Like a picture, a metaphor is a way of saying something which cannot be encompassed by words. The terms, primate and metaprimate, as I have used them are metaphors. At both ends they open into a space where words are a hindrance. Poetry helps. It mystifies.

What does it mean to be more than man? The me-thou dichotomy is the basis of biological life. To be an organism is to be sense-oriented—to believe in the evidence of the senses, to feed on matter, to perceive within the limitations of the senses and consider these perceptions as final. The me-thou dichotomy is part of this sensorily perceived world. Within the limitations of our senses we perceive form. We sense ourselves. We sense others. There is a clear distinction. We like ourselves—this form that we perceive as ourself. To sustain this form we require food in material form and other material resources. We perceive these as limited. The material world is a finite world. We are afflicted by a sense of scarcity—by a need to compete, control, own, fight, fear. For other organisms the scarcity is real. For us it is imagined, *assumed* by our primate-human mind.

We have misunderstood ourselves. I have tried to show in this book that our senses are designed in a particular way to reveal to us the world in a particular form. There is nothing absolute about this form. The me-thou or me-it or it-it dichotomy is an artifact of the senses.

Spirituality and love are not different things. Both challenge the me-thou, and in their final form, me-it dichotomy. *Our greatest moments are those in which we meet with each other and with the world on a plane above the me-thou or me-it dichotomy.* These are usually brief moments. But they leave a taste. And then we begin to do it more and more. We find people with whom we can have these meetings. It is easier with some but it is always available with *everyone* when we know how. And only we know how.

Behind sensory experience is episensory experience. When perception gets stuck on the sensory, as it almost always does, we evaluate, interpret, judge on the basis of likes and dislikes spawned by the me-thou dichotomy. We see a white man or a black man, a rich man or a poor man. We evaluate, feel and respond according to concepts, judgments, generalisations. A young child, unencumbered by these, is open to the episensory experience of the person, open to a more authentic meeting.

Those who are able to latch on, consciously or unconsciously, to those moments or periods of contact where the me-thou dichotomy is suspended can get addicted to the experience. It then becomes difficult to accommodate to the primate-human world. We experience "spirit blues"—a pulling down to a lower vibration of consciousness. Then we try to escape, take drugs, despair of humanity—its brutal wars, cruelty, injustice, ecological destruction, greed, fear, exploitation.

But when we understand where the human species is coming from and where it is trying to go the picture, and our reactions to it, change. *Given from where we have come*, why should we be any different? We are deeply primate, powerfully controlled by genetic programs billions of years old. These are unconscious. They keep us trapped in primate behaviour, evidence of which is seen daily in the newspapers and on television.

Individually and collectively we are engaged in an unconscious struggle to become more than "man". Here, "man", used metaphorically, ironically becomes a symbol of the primate-human and the difference between men and women is highlighted. Women have a greater natural ability to become more than man. They are more evolved, less trapped in primate psychology. In a man's world they are constantly pulled down.

As we, individually, become more than man, a wonderful thing happens. We begin to meet each other and the world in a way unknown to primate man. We find that there is no two.

We don't need Sufism or Buddhism or Christianity to show us how to do this.

———————————

A.D. 2000: A Mathnawi in English

Note: Technically speaking, a Mathnawi, in Urdu and
Farsi, is a heroic poem, or a poem which tells a tale or a series of
tales, and is composed in precise rhyme and metre. But it can
also be a "teaching poem", like Rumi's Mathnawi. The ability of
poetry to communicate much more that what is said in so many
words is well recognised. The use of metaphor, allegory, symbol
and simile is a universal feature of poetry, but Farsi and Urdu
classical poets have elevated it to a high art. Sufi poets, such as
Rumi and Hafiz, have repeatedly made deliberate use of such
artifices to convey "hidden" truths and yet maintain their sacred
and secret nature so that only the most discerning seekers would
be privy to the knowledge so communicated. The poem which
follows employs no such artifices. It would be meaningless to
transplant oriental symbols and literary delicacies into the body
of a western language, especially English, whose structure and
articulation are designed for functionality rather than a dance.
On the other hand, the relative directness of style which
characterises communication, even poetic communication, in
English has outstanding advantages if the objective is to make
the knowledge more widely available. I am convinced that the
world needs a wider communication of this knowledge and a
large number of people (though their percentage is small) are
indeed ready for it. I am simply passing on, in mine own flawed
words, what I have learnt and understood.

The question keeps gnawing
Demanding, as it were, a whole new game
From the one that has been played
Ever since it began
With no discernible intention
And became what it became.
The question keeps gnawing
What are we going to do, my friend,
When nothing is left to do but more of the same?
More of the same as spinning out webs of greed,
Eating up nature, having a good time,
Putting each other down,

Or being kind to other animals.
More of the same
As going to vote and choosing every few years
The same woman or man with a different name.
More of the same
As filling the hole
In the centre of the soul
With the same old everyday shame.
More of the same as playing a game of Scrabble
And hoping to find in the scrambled letters
The meaning of the game.
The question is haunting
What are we going to do, my friend,
Now that nothing is left to do
But more of the same, more of the same, more of the same?

••••

Shouldn't we have seen it coming?
But then we are hardly to blame
We followed the book we were given
The one someone else had written
And flawlessly played the game.
A single checkmate would have done the job
But move after move is made
And all the moves come out the same
Is there no way to end the game?

••••

There is a way, my friend,
But first you must know
What is the game and who is the player
You move the pieces
And you think you are making the moves
Ha! Ha! Think again
You think the game is about winning
Grabbing the biggest piece of cake
Hands are for grabbing, are they not? you say
But look what happens when you have had your cake
You are hungry again.

••••

The game is contrived, my friend,
The cake is an illusion
And the hunger doesn't exist
Except in your heart
What cake would fill that empty space?

••••

You are a place where illusions take place
The cake doesn't exist any more than you do
Your brain is an organ where energy gets coiled
And freezes for a second as it tries to decide
Which way to go, what neural path to take
(No other animal has this luxury to pause)
And in this frozen moment when life stops to look at itself
Arises the phantom Self, the I, as you call it
Which begins to invest so fiercely
In its unreal reality
That it appropriates to itself
The thoughts and fears, passions and sensations of the organism
Within whose brain it has arisen like a phantom
They then become "my" thoughts, "my" fears, "my" passions, "my"
sensations
I begin to exist as the imaginary owner
Of "my" thoughts, "my" feelings, "my" desires
What happens then is the beginning of sorrow
What happens is that we separate from Life
From the Life that flows through the organism
Unselfconscious, like a current, doing its thing.
Watch, for a moment, a year-old child
It takes no credit or blame
For what it thinks or what it does
There is no one there yet to lay claim
To Life's activities
The child is free and one with Life
Free, that is, until we step in
And teach it the game of credit and blame and ownership
And, of course, shame.

••••

The mechanics of liberation are far simpler
Than the coiled chains

Which bind the mind's I
It goes round and round in a convoluted trap
Appropriating this, laying claim to that
"I own therefore I am"
This body is mine, as are these thoughts and deeds
This is my wife, my husband, my child
Do I not have legal rights to all these things?
So lines are drawn and markers go up
Territories defined, boundaries laid out
Wars are fought, people compete
To fill their hands with loot
The phantom Self survives by owning
Or rather, the delusion of owning,
That which is owned by neither God nor man
If Life could be owned
It would turn to stone.

••••

Do you not long to be free
To enjoy Life's sensuousness to its uttermost delight?
The gifts of the Spirit
And the love, oh the love,
Which moment to moment
Breathes Life into us?
Then cease from appropriating
That which is not yours.

••••

How long, dear God, will it take us to learn
What every child knows?
Life's sensuousness requires neither wealth nor power
To partake of
It is there, every moment
Like a nipple to be sucked, like lips to be kissed
A breast to be fondled, a wound to be licked
A mind to be expanded, a poem to be birthed
Life happens through us and not due to us.

••••

"I own therefore I am"
Is how the Self knows itself
And establishes its unreal reality

You may own your house, yes,
That's man's law, a legal convention
To organise society's affairs
From this you surmise
That Life can be chopped up
And chunks of it captured, appropriated, owned.
This poem is created by Life
Not by Ali Ansari
There is no Ali Ansari
He never existed.
Except by mutual agreement

••••

Man's law and God's law are things apart
The one is convention, the other is truth
Disown all that is not yours
Until nothing is left
No owner, no ownership, no self
Just the sense of this incredibly sensuous flow of Life
And Love's Kindly Breath blowing gently on the face
Oh, the joy and freedom of disowning everything.
No one can own you then
Not even you
Just think WHAT you will be when you have given up all.

Bibliography

Note: Almost all the books listed here are relatively non-technical and easy to read. I have not included journal papers. I have also not included titles on Sufism, since I have not referred to any in the course of the writing. Of the books I have seen I do not find any outstanding enough to single out and recommend. Sufism must be lived, not read.

Introduction

1. Ansari, A., *Higher-order Energy And Information Spaces: A Conceptual Framework* (privately published, 1979).
2. Eddington, A.S., *The Nature of the Physical World* (Macmillan, 1928).
3. Le Doux, J.. *The Emotional Brain* (Simon & Schuster, 1996).
4. Ramachandran, V.S. and Blakeslee, S., *Phantoms In The Brain* (4th Estate, 1998)

A Note About Sufi And New Sufi Thought

1. Scott, Ernst, *The People of the Secret* (Octagon Press, 1983).
2. Gold, E.J., *The Human Biological Machine As A Transformational Apparatus* (Gateways,'86)

Chapter 1

1. Humphrey, N., *A History of the Mind* (Simon & Schuster, 1992)
2. Crick, Francis, *The Astonishing Hypothesis* (Touchstone,1994).
3. Dossey, L., *Space, Time And Medicine* (Shambhala,1982).
4. Sacks,O., *An Anthropologist on Mars* (Picador,1995).
5. Gal-Or, B., ed., *Modern Developments In Thermodynamics* (Academic Press,1973).

6. Behe, M., *Darwin's Black Box* (Touchstone.1998).
7. Simeons, A.T.W., *Man's Presumptuous Brain* (Dutton,1962).
8. Pert, Candace, *Molecules of Emotion* (Scribner,1997).

Chapter 2

1. Wilson, E.O., *Consilience—The Unity of Knowledge* (A.A. Knopf,1998).
2. Capra, F., *The Web of Life* (Harper Collins,1997).

Chapter 4

1. Churchland, Patricia S., *Neurophilosophy* (Bradford Books, M.I.T., 1986).
2. Ramachandran, V.S., ibid.
3. Sacks, O., ibid.
4. Crick, Francis, ibid.
5. Penrose, R., *Shadows of the Mind* (Vintage, 1995).
6. "What Is Enlightenment?" Fall/Winter 1998 issue (Moksha Press, Lenox, MA, USA).

Chapter 5

1. I AM THAT: Talks With Nisargadatta Maharaj (Acorn Press, Durham, N.C. 1996).

Chapter 8

1. Scott, E., ibid.
2. Gold. E.J., ibid.

Chapter 12

1. Sacks,O. ibid.
2. Ramachandran. V.S. ibid.
3. Pert, C., ibid.

Love

They think love needs an object of love
A man, woman or a thing
In their love there are always two
A lover and a beloved.
They do not know that love is present
Only when there is no two
And that is only possible
When there is no one
When the lover has gone back
Whence she came

NOTE

Anyone wishing to set up a website to enable readers of this book to share thoughts, reactions, reflections is welcome to do so. But please consult me before doing so.